# TEACHING ART
# AT KEY STAGE 2

Nigel Meager

Julie Ashfield

VISUAL IMPACT PUBLICATIONS

NSEAD
NATIONAL SOCIETY FOR EDUCATION IN ART & DESIGN

Photography: Nigel Meager, Julie Ashfield,
Stephen Verbeeck, Welsh Folk Museum Library.
Photographs developed and printed by Collier's
Photographic Emporium, Uplands, Swansea

Designed by Andy Dark, Cardiff
Printed by Pensord Press, Blackwood
Imaging by Ideas Into Print, Gower

First Published in 1995 by NSEAD and
Visual Impact Publications
Reprinted 1997
Reprinted 2000
Distributed by NSEAD
The Gatehouse,
Corsham Court,
Corsham,
Wiltshire,
SN13 OBZ

ISBN 0 904684 20 2

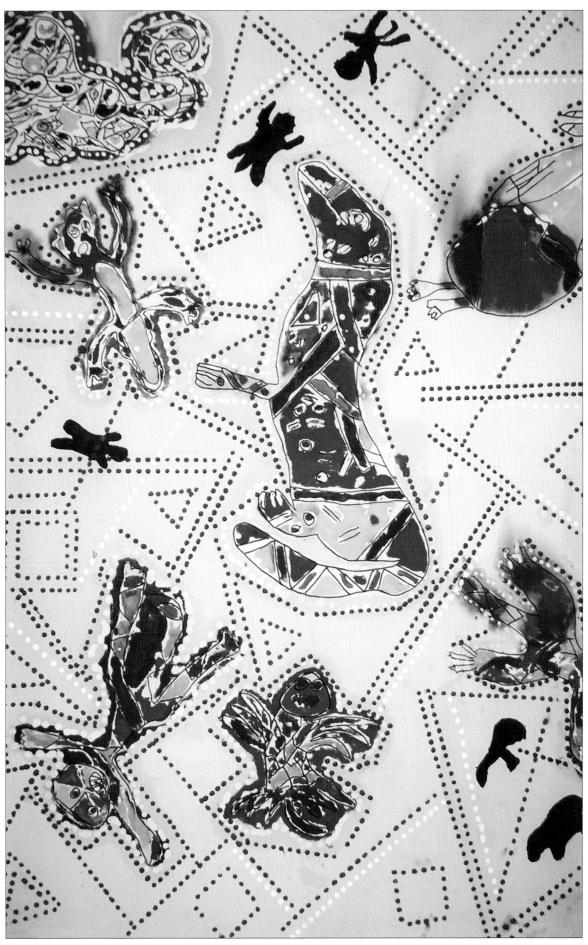

Group work inspired by visiting an art gallery (see page 99)

**Nigel Meager**

Nigel trained as an artist, completing an MA in Fine Art in 1985. Since then he has been working in many different ways with primary school teachers and children. Nigel is committed to demystifying art and has worked to develop art projects for the primary classroom that are accessible for the teacher who is not a specialist in art. As well as working regularly in the classroom with children, Nigel runs in-service education courses for schools and local education authorities and is invited to speak at conferences across the UK. This reprinted edition complements 'Teaching Art at Key Stage 1' also available from NSEAD. Nigel's other publications include a series of handbooks written for parents and teachers who work with children in the early years. The books are published for Crayola® and are called 'Teaching Your Children Art'.

**Julie Ashfield** is the advisory teacher for art in Cardiff. Nigel Meager and Julie Ashfield collaborated to write the South Glamorgan planning guidelines for art in the National Curriculum. The advice on planning in the introduction to this book is based upon that work. Julie supported the publication of 'Teaching Art at Key Stage 2' by researching appropriate examples of contemporary practice in South Glamorgan Schools as part of her MA in Art and Design Education at University of Wales Institute, Cardiff.

Making patterns in the environment

# Contents

## Preface

## Introduction

## Illustrating stories and working with an artist

## Pattern, different cultures and IT

# Jungles

# Landscape drawings and paintings

# Portraits 5

# Figure drawing 6

# Figures and heads in clay 7

# Drawing buildings 8

# Abstraction, construction and relief printing | 3

# Sarajevo, war and fear | 4

# Conclusion | 5

# Materials and resources list | 6

# Index | 7

## 'Teaching Art at Key Stage 1'

'Teaching Art at Key Stage 2' has been written as a sequel to 'Teaching art at Key Stage 1', published by the National Society for Education in Art and Design and Visual Impact Publications in 1993. This sequel, like 'Teaching Art at Key Stage 1', is a book for primary school teachers.

'Teaching Art at Key Stage 1' developed out of the Visual Impact Project in West Glamorgan. This project allowed artists to work in the classroom with primary school children. A partnership between the artist and teacher led to a sharing of professional expertise and improved strategies for teaching art. The project was initiated in 1988 and ran until 1992. At the time the idea was innovative and won support from the Calouste Gulbenkian Foundation, West Glamorgan Education Authority and the Welsh Arts Council. The Calouste Gulbenkian Foundation went on to support the publication of 'Teaching Art at Key Stage 1'.

In 'Teaching Art at Key Stage 1' each of the eight chapters has as its theme one of the visual concepts that make up the visual language of art, craft and design. The chapter headings are Shape, Pattern, Colour, Form, Space, Tone, Texture and Line and Mark. The intention was to provide a wealth of practical ideas which were more than merely 'tips for teachers'. An important premise was that what is actually said to children matters. Therefore the text was written partly in the form of a dialogue that recorded precisely what might be said to young children by the class teacher.

The activities described in 'Teaching Art at Key Stage 1' build one on another. A typical sequence begins with discussion and is followed by ideas to help children experiment and explore one or other of the visual concepts, children go on to learn or revise a process, technique or skill and then finish by making an art craft or design object. Woven into the text are ideas about how teachers can encourage children to talk about art. 'Teaching Art at Key Stage 2' follows a similar pattern.

## The relationship between 'Teaching Art at Key Stage 1' and 'Teaching Art at Key Stage 2'

Whereas in 'Teaching Art at Key Stage 1' the visual elements provided the chapter headings, the chapters in 'Teaching Art at Key Stage 2' are a series of project examples. The implication is that at Key Stage 2 the formal strategies for developing the visual language of art (work with colour, tone, texture etc.) are more likely to be integrated into projects that progressively open up potential for both breadth and depth in the children's art and design. Any underlying planning strategy (one is described in the introduction), must include a number of features that interact with the formal elements. In many cases the formal elements themselves become subsumed into projects that might have as a focus a range of features such as language, imagination, ideas, skills and examples of adult art.

In 'Teaching Art at Key Stage 2' the chapters are not intended to form a prescriptive system or scheme of work, rather they can be used to prompt ideas for units of work appropriate to individual schools. No attempt is made in this book to suggest a particular scheme of work that is to be progressively introduced through Years 3,4, 5 and 6. Although teachers might face pressure to plan an art programme rather like a maths scheme works, because the nature of art and design is so broad and because the individual art experience of individual children and schools is so diverse, it is inappropriate to write a scheme or programme that might work for each and every case. The idea behind this book is to show as clearly as possible a set of examples of how art and design might be taught. It must be the responsibility of each teacher and school to work out art projects that are sensitive to the particular context of child, class, school and curriculum so that the projects will be appropriate to the needs of the children that they teach. However, most primary teachers are not art specialists, many gave up art before 'O' level or GCSE, and any book that purports to support the teaching of art in primary schools must recognise this fact. Within each chapter there is much specific advice on teaching aspects of an art curriculum to primary age children.

'Teaching Art at Key Stage 1' advocated the value of teaching a foundation of basic skills and concepts. An implication for Key Stage 2 is that if children have already been introduced to both the visual language of art and to a set of core skills at Key Stage 1, they will be able to progress towards more sophisticated art work. The importance of providing a foundation of work at Key Stage 1 cannot be over emphasised.

Not all children at Key Stage 2 will have this foundation of skills and concepts in place. For example, many teachers will recognise that Year 6 classes lack experience in National Curriculum Art. One of the issues is often that the kind of activities appropriate at Key Stage 1 are equally suitable for Key Stage 2. In practice all the activities

Modelling an imaginary creature in clay, Year 6

from the book 'Teaching Art at Key Stage 1' could be used at Key Stage 2, with the proviso that the language used in the classroom may change and older children will grasp concepts more quickly and work rapidly through some of the less demanding activities. One way of thinking about this is to use the activities described in 'Teaching Art at Key Stage 1' as starting points for the more advanced projects that will challenge children in Key Stage 2. In fact the activities in 'Teaching Art at Key Stage 1' become warm up exercises and a way of revising basic concepts and skills for many of the projects in this book. Teachers who are already familiar with 'Teaching Art at Key Stage 1' will recognise the content of these warm up exercises and starting points. Because there is a natural overlap between the two books there is inevitably some repetition. This is essential in order to place the work at Key Stage 2 in the context of what preceded at Key Stage 1. The overlap also

allows teachers who have not read 'Teaching Art at Key Stage 1' to fully implement the Key Stage 2 projects described in this publication.

So the relationship between the two volumes is a balance between the educational need for continuity including more advanced progressive projects for Key Stage 2 and the recognition that children at Key Stage 2 may still be working at a level more appropriate to Key Stage 1. 'Teaching Art at Key Stage 2' also reflects the heartening and increasing number of contemporary examples of advanced and sophisticated art teaching for Key Stage 2. All the projects have been tried and tested in the classroom. Because of this there is a detailed description of how a number of examples of primary art projects work.

## Planning the projects

There are a number of possible ways in which art activities for primary school children could be organised. The planning that preceded the projects in 'Teaching Art at Key Stage 2' took into account the most important of these:

1.  the visual concepts
2.  the theme, topic or stimulus (that is the subject of the art activity)
3.  the processes and skills which are used to make the art, craft or design object
4.  the examples of art, craft and design that are introduced to children in order to help build their knowledge and understanding of art

Diagram 'A' shows each of these as four possible components that could help plan the kinds of primary art projects illustrated in this book. Each of the chapters is subdivided into a number of potential working sessions and each session has its own subheading. These subheadings have been coded to show under which of the four main components from diagram 'A' the session could be placed. In some cases there may be more than one possibility. This may give teachers an insight into how the projects were planned and developed. This should also highlight that the relationship between the four components is complex and does not reduce to a simple formula where 'a' always follows 'b'. This is an advantage as it allows for rich, varied and individual project structures. Teachers will immediately see different ways of combining elements of the work into units appropriate for their own class and school.

DIAGRAM A

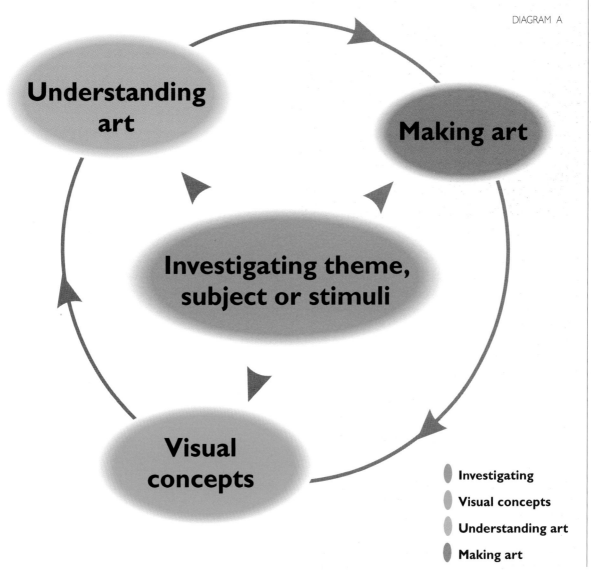

Understanding art

Making art

Investigating theme, subject or stimuli

Visual concepts

- Investigating
- Visual concepts
- Understanding art
- Making art

Still life painting, Year 6

## Art in the National Curriculum

Diagram 'A' illustrates this way of interpreting art, craft and design in the National Curriculum. The diagram is particularly appropriate to National Curriculum Art in either England or Wales. The word 'art' is used as a short form of the phrase 'art, craft and design' in the English and Welsh orders. In this book 'art' should also be taken to mean 'art and design' or 'art, craft and design'. In the text the word 'art' and the phrases 'art and design' and 'art, craft and design' are interchanged at will.

The curriculum structure in both Scotland and Northern Ireland is different. ' Art and Design' is used in both Scotland and Northern Ireland as part of a wider collection of subjects that feature expression and creativity as part of an arts rather than visual art curriculum. However teachers in Scotland and Northern Ireland will recognise that the spirit of their curriculum documents for art and design are still reflected in diagram 'A'. The diagram will illuminate both the Scottish 'strands' that include the concepts of using media, investigating, using visual elements and reflecting, describing and responding to works of art as well as the developing Curriculum Order for Northern

Ireland that has included the concepts of investigating and realising. Giving practical help to teachers in using some underlying concepts that lead to effective art and design projects is relevant no matter which of the four different United Kingdom art documents is used as a bench mark for the art, craft and design curriculum.

The inner central oval of diagram 'A' suggests the need to consider which themes, subjects or stimuli might provide the starting point for art. In most of the projects described in this book children begin by investigating stimuli that the teacher has provided or pointed out. This approach is intentionally cross-curricular. Some examples of thematic or subject based starting points might include 'Ourselves', 'Shapes in Maths', 'Buildings and the Built Environment', 'Patterns and Fabrics', 'Materials in Science'. There will be many other starting points. Questions arise such as: Is there a possibility of providing a visual stimulus inside the classroom for the children? Is it appropriate to take them outside, perhaps outside school? How are the children going to investigate the subject? Will there be opportunities for making collections of relevant objects and images? Will there be opportunities for the children to record information about the subject? Can they explore the stimulus in different ways? A teacher might encourage the use of a camera. Sketchbooks will be used. A collection of library books might help. A display of some kind is almost inevitable. The children could investigate the stimulus using one or more appropriate visual elements. The quality of the stimuli will excite and inspire children.

Spinning around the inner oval are boxes that show three more important facets that could be taken into account when planning a series of art activities. A number of the most fundamental visual concepts (they are sometimes called visual elements) can be listed as colour, shape, pattern, tone, texture, form, space and line (the concept of 'mark' is sometimes coupled with line). Paying attention to one or more of these concepts as part of a project will not only provide part of the focus for the children's investigations of the theme, but also help structure both their making and their talking about art, craft and design. Working within a framework of the visual concepts will help to develop children's visual perception. It is an inevitable consequence that the children will need to experiment and work with a range of media appropriate to the exploration of different visual concepts.

Guiding children towards an understanding of art will involve introducing them to different examples of art, craft and design. It will be important that they have the opportunity to talk about these examples. Over a period of time children should encounter art, craft and design from different cultures, both contemporary and historical. Use examples of art that connect with the relevant theme or stimuli, illustrate visual concepts and are examples of processes used in making. For example, teachers may choose to show children patterned fabrics as part of a pattern project or perhaps two different portraits because the class theme is 'ourselves'. The children can explore these examples focusing on one of the visual concepts such as pattern, colour or shape. Children can go on to make their own art as a response to examples to which they have been introduced. The teacher may give the children factual information to help develop knowledge about appropriate art, as well as about the artists, craftsworkers and designers themselves.

Through the investigation of a subject or theme, work with an appropriate visual concept and talk about relevant art, children will have many ideas that will stimulate them to make their own art, craft and design. It is best if these ideas are the children's own discoveries and have come out of the quality of experience that the teacher has structured. It is all to easy to give the children your

ideas and even to go on and do the work for them! There are many examples of primary school art that are billed as children's work but in reality most of the ideas and a fair proportion of the execution was dominated by an adult's influence. There is a fine line to be drawn here. It is not easy to step back and let children make all their own creative decisions. It might be impractical to do so, because children also look for help and need guidance. Much primary art is actually a collaboration between adult direction and children's own creative input.

If the children are to go on to express their ideas as art they will need to be able to use one or more of a number of processes and skills. They

Sculptural construction, Year 6

will need some basic training in how to use certain equipment and materials so that they can work creatively without getting in a muddle or a mess. A basic list of skills and process the children should experience includes: using a sketchbook, observational and imaginative drawing, design drawing (planning the way something is going to look), painting (colour mixing skills), using pastels and crayons, printing, collage, using clay, sculptural construction, working with fabrics and threads and using a computer (to help with design). Processes do not have to become more complex as the children get older. A simple relief print can be as relevant to a mature artist as to a child in Year 3. It is far more important to ensure a continuity of art experience as the children develop through the primary school. Many of the basic skills learnt at Key Stage 1 can be repeated at Key Stage 2 where older children will develop a more sophisticated response as they find themselves more at ease with a familiar way of working. If teachers wish to use more complex processes these can be developed from a firm understanding of basic ones. It is tempting to think that a progressive scheme of work will mean that pupils in Year 5 and 6 should be experience more complicated ways of making art. This is not necessarily true.

An art activity is unlikely to be a one-off affair. Work which has meaning and quality often will come from a project that is built from a series of related activities involving all the four components: investigating a stimulus, working with one or more visual concepts, talking about examples of art, craft and design and using one or more appropriate processes and skills. The circular nature of diagram 'A' shows how the four areas should not be considered separately when planning art projects. Rather, all the activities interweave and feed off one another.

Diagram 'B' provides a summary of the above discussion.

## Other factors which may be taken into consideration when planning projects

Diagram C shows some of the other factors that may be taken into account when planning the kinds of projects illustrated in this book. Use the phrases as reminders of factors that must be taken into consideration.when planning projects. There is no intended hierarchy here, any of these factors may assume a greater or lesser importance depending on the specific content of each project. They are included to help teachers consider some of the more general implications of the National Curriculum for Art and its interpretation in contemporary primary art practice.

## Achieving an overview of art education in a primary school

Diagram D provides one example of how it is possible to see at a glance the balance of some of the components that make up art, craft and design education in a school. The headings within the diagram indicate a focus for each term of work. The headings are not exclusive, much more art activity may also happen during the term. However it is possible to use an agreed planning map such as this to ensure that at least the minimum entitlement is taught and that the curriculum allows for both breadth and continuity.

DIAGRAM B

# Building a Foundation

### Investigate the stimulus theme or topic

Ourselves, portraits, hair styles and hats, houses, architecture, gardens, the beach, natural and man made materials, clothing and fabrics, Victorian patterns, jewellery and body ornaments, colour, shadows, the rain forest, plants and leaves, water and reflections, the farm, structures, inventions, movement, machines, shapes, figures, games, forces, electricity, a picnic, weddings and celebrations, birthdays, fear and war, trapped, table-top collections and many others ...
Explore, record, make collections, use a sketchbook, take photographs, work with appropriate visual concepts ...

| **Work with concepts** | **Talk about art, craft and design** | **Introduce skills and processes** |
|---|---|---|
| **explore and experiment with the visual elements using different media and techniques** | **building knowledge and understanding** | **making art** |
| Shape | Introduce children to examples and encourage a response through discussion and the children's own practical work | Drawing in a sketchbook |
| Pattern | | Drawing from observation |
| Colour | Our culture | Drawing designs |
| Form | Other cultures | Painting |
| Space | The past | Working with pastels and crayons |
| Texture | Now | Printing |
| Tone | this includes working with artists and visiting galleries | Collage |
| Line and Mark | | Using clay |
| | | Construction |
| | | Fabrics & threads |
| | | Using a computer |

### Pulling it all together

Can you plan a sequence of activities that integrate the four areas? This will build into a project over several weeks. There will be a number of projects each year. Do these projects include work in both two and three dimensions? Are children using their imaginations and working from their own past experience as well as direct observation? Plan for work that may involve groups, the whole class and individual children. This work may be in a variety of scales using a range of materials, tools and techniques. Value and display examples of all the work, including the experimental and investigative.

DIAGRAM C

children will learn about artists from Wales

the scheme of work will be balanced, progressive and allow for children of all abilities and needs

children will be able to mix colours

children will work as individuals, in groups on small, medium and large scale projects

children will learn about artists from different cultures and different periods in history

the children will explore the visual elements of art, craft and design

children will work with line, tone, pattern, texture, shape, form and space

the children will be involved in collecting and organising visual and tactile material of all kinds

the children will learn a range of different skills

children will be able to talk about art, including their own art

children will learn about how to organise and care for equipment and materials

the children will find out about the world around them, including the world of their imaginations

children will use a sketchbook at Key Stage Two

children will learn about local artists

children will be able to plan for and modify their work

the children will make their own response to the work of others

children will work with information technology

there will be a balance between work in two and three dimensions

the children will be introduced to a range of examples of art, craft and design

children will learn to work safely

children will be given opportunities to explore and experiment

DIAGRAM D

|  | Nursery | Reception | Year 1 | Year 2 | Year 3 | Year 4 | Year 5 | Year 6 | Year 7 |
|---|---|---|---|---|---|---|---|---|---|
| TERM 1 |  | Colour<br><br>Painting<br><br>Autumn | Shape<br><br>Collage<br><br>Landscape | Tone<br><br>Drawing<br><br>Light | Colour<br><br>Painting<br><br>Autumn | Shape<br><br>Drawing<br><br>People | Space<br><br>Construction<br><br>Theatre | Form<br><br>Clay<br><br>War |  |
| TERM 2 |  | Texture<br><br>Clay<br><br>Materials | Line<br><br>Fabrics<br><br>Ourselves | Space<br><br>Painting<br><br>Spring | Texture<br><br>Construction<br><br>Outer space | Line<br><br>Printing<br><br>Journeys | Pattern<br><br>Fabrics<br><br>World | Texture<br><br>Drawing<br><br>Seashore |  |
| TERM 3 |  | Pattern<br><br>Printing<br><br>Houses | Form<br><br>Construction<br><br>Machines | Pattern<br><br>Printing<br><br>Celebrations | Form<br><br>Clay<br><br>Celts | Tone<br><br>Collage<br><br>Animals | Colour<br><br>Painting<br><br>Food | Shape<br><br>Printing<br><br>Victorians |  |

## Drafting a policy - some possible headings

- Broad Aims - match these to those of the school and education authority or education board if appropriate

- Subject Aims - general - include gender, multicultural and special needs issues here

- A statement about the existing strengths and tradition of art education in the school

- Statement of link to National Curriculum or guidelines. General requirements, programmes of study and end of key stage descriptions are acknowledged

- How schemes and units of work are planned

- Art and design skills and processes to be taught

- Visual language teaching (visual elements)

- Examples of art, craft and design to be introduced

- Appropriate teaching styles (class, group or individual work)

- Opportunities to work across the curriculum

- Display in the classroom and school enviroment

- Links to home

- Information Technology

- Visits to galleries, working with artists, community arts projects

- Continuity and links between Key Stages - awareness of Key Stage 3

- Differentiation

- Recording and Assessment

- Health and safety

- In-service training

- Regular audits of staff skills and available materials and resources

## A policy for Art

Diagram E suggests some possible paragraph headings for a school policy for art education. Each school in each education authority or education board will need to tailor a policy for their individual circumstances.

## Reading 'Teaching Art at Key Stage 2'

Read through one of the chapters to get a feel for how the book is written. There are different voices running through the text. There is the voice of the teacher talking to the children:

> "Now look for shadows. Start by drawing in the very darkest tones. Then add in more shadows and tones from each part of the head."

There is the voice of the author giving advice and information to the teacher:

"Pick a selection of portraits by adult artists to show the children. Postcards are useful for group work. But you may need larger prints if you wish to talk about the portraits with the whole class."

There is also information about materials and equipment that might be used for an activity:

**Materials and Resources:**
Charcoal and chalk
Large sheets of paper
An easel or flip chart
Drawing boards
Hair spray

Each chapter is an example of a project or unit of work that may be planned to take place over a period of many weeks, some projects might last a whole term. The individual subheadings give some indication of how a teacher might divide the project into a series of sessions or lessons. In many cases teachers will need to select from the sessions to build a project appropriate for their own class. There are many variables within each class and school, there are also many different teaching styles that can contribute to a successful art project. Please use the projects as prompts, pointers and examples to help plan your own approach. Please resist the temptation to follow each chapter through as a fixed recipe for success.

It is intended that the individual sessions build one on another to create a developing set of ideas that grow in richness and sophistication.

Teachers may question whether the projects are designed for specific year groups or age ranges. The answer to this question is 'no'. All the projects, with the possible exception of the final chapter, 'Sarajevo, War and Fear', can be adapted for any year group at Key Stage 2. It is a feature of art education that progression does not necessarily involve increasingly sophisticated and complex activities. Exploring ideas in a sketchbook may be as appropriate to a student working towards an MA in Fine Art as it is to a Year 3 child in primary school.

## Use the illustrations

Illustrations have been carefully selected to enhance the text. In many cases the photographs contain a great deal of useful information and they will reward careful study. Wherever possible the photographs have been placed close to relevant text. Images have been chosen both for their content and for their graphic power. Much of the illustrated work is intended to inspire and reflects the achievment of excellence by children at Key Stage 2.

Imaginative collage, Year 4

Landscape painting, Year 5

## Use the index and table of contents

You may be planning an art project and, for example, discover that you need specific advice on an approach to shape and form. The project involves design work that you would like to develop further using clay. Use the index to locate references to these italicised words in the text. Glance through the table of contents. Are there any subheadings within a chapter that might link with the work you are planning? Although this book cannot claim to cover every possible aspect of teaching art at Key Stage 2 many basic approaches to teaching a range of skills and concepts are covered within the various chapters. The subheadings in the table of contents also provide an at a glance indication of how each project develops.

## Making Art Work

Teaching Art at Key Stage 1' and now 'Teaching Art at Key Stage 2' grew out of a conviction that it is possible to talk simply and clearly about art. Artists and art teachers often appear to surround their activity in a haze of mystery. To these art specialists art is so esoteric and difficult that it is

better, more honest, not to say too much. Words get in the way of the art. For some art specialists it is almost as if art is magical and that to participate in 'real' art you must possess special gifts and insights.

Practising a collage technique

So for many primary teachers it seems as if no one has ever stopped to take the time to talk simply and clearly about art. It is probable during their initial teacher training comparatively little time had been set aside to help teachers teach art. It is not surprising that in the classroom some teachers either avoided teaching the subject or resorted to prescriptive stencils and formulas that were easy to follow and generated passable end products. Yet art, craft and design surround us the whole of our lives. We should be able to talk about art in the same down to earth way we discuss any other human activity. Art is not a necessarily difficult and obscure activity: it touches our lives in very direct ways.

The most down to earth way of suggesting how art can work for young children is to describe what may be said by their teacher as the activity is introduced and developed in the classroom. The words attain even greater significance if the visual results of the activities are presented along side. It is a feature of this book that a great many photographs of children and their art work are seen together with a detailed description of the projects concerned. These descriptions include an emphasis on what might actually be said by the teacher to the class. It is not necessary or effective to use jargon or to postulate slogans when working with primary age children. The intention here is to show that art is simple, accessible and thoroughly teachable.

Art can be demystified. The principle is to pay attention to the particular rather than attempt to work in terms of general definitions and models. It is the particular nature of art that is its strength. Art allows individual children to physically reach out towards the world that surrounds and is within them. Children react to this world. This reaction can be through an art activity like drawing. The drawing is their response to the world. Children feel the power of having succeeded in capturing the physical world in a physical medium. This reaction, this expression, is not abstract or esoteric, neither is it a definable system or set of slogans, it is as real as each sense of touch or sensation of smell, it is as intense as a strong colour. Children feel the power of the sensation of being alive, they are conscious of 'self'. They are inspired to work. Art gives them this and it is as natural, as straightforward and as particular as their individual words and deeds.

Exploring line

An illustration of fear (see page 118), Year 6

# Illustrating stories and working with an artist

Drawing the dragon (see page 24), Year 3

## ❶ Starting with a story

This is a short unit of work that developed out of a literature project based upon a story from Terry Jones' book, 'Fantastic Stories'.

Read the story to the children:
A family is very frightened because a large dragon

Starting with a story

lands on the roof of their home. They seek help from a rather stupid emperor. He enlists the support of a number dragon slayers to try and get rid of the dragon. The truth is that all the dragon is doing is resting before he flies away to die. The best dragon slayers tell the emperor to leave the dragon alone, he will do no harm. However, the emperor is hoping to curry favour with the people who are frightened. A young dragon slayer sees the opportunity for fame and volunteers to kill the dragon. It will be an easy task. The dragon slayer shoots the dragon in the eye and in the side. This causes a devastating effect on the surrounding landscape as the blood and innards of the dragon spill out. The dragon tells the dragon slayer, "I don't mean any harm, I just want to be left to die." The dragon defends himself with his last breath of fire, but in the end he dies. The dragon is dead and much of the countryside is ruined but the emperor and dragon slayers are heroes.

The children are fascinated by the fate of the dragon. The story is discussed.

**"What do think about how the dragon has been treated? What was the dragon feeling? How would**

you have felt if you were the dragon? How would you feel if the dragon landed on your roof? Have you ever felt persecuted? Have you ever been in a situation that is unfair?"

Materials and Resources:
A story from Terry Jones' book 'Fantastic Stories'.

### ❯Drawing the dragon

Drawing the dragon

This is drawing from the imagination. It might be better if the children do not see illustrations of the dragon before they make their own drawings.

> "Think about the size of the dragon, he fills the whole roof top, he is very large. Think about what the dragon looks like. What are the most noticable features of the dragon? Remember the descriptions in the story. Remember the nostrils, the eyes, the teeth! There is no need to draw the whole dragon. For example, you could draw just the head and neck.
>
> You will be working on the drawing boards and you will have large sheets of paper. Think big, big paper,

big drawings! To help, you can use these marker pens. They make strong dark lines."

The children could make some quick rough drawings in their sketchbooks to help them come up with an idea.

Prop the boards up along a corridor or in the hall for an informal exhibition. Talk about the differences in the children's dragons.

Materials and Resources:
Sketchbooks
Drawing media
Drawing boards and masking tape
Large sheets of paper, A2 size
Black or coloured marker pens

### ❯❯Mr and Mrs Twit or Stig of the Dump

This is another illustration project that used Roald Dahl's book 'The Twits' as a focus. One of the illustrations shows an example of work from one child who worked in a similar way with the character of Stig from the novel 'Stig of the Dump'. In this project the imaginative work is preceded by investigative work on tone and mark. Although the text refers to the Twits, the project will work just as well using the character of Stig. In the previous example you may wish to support the children's dragon drawings by helping children explore the concept of shape before they draw, look at page 79 for advice about focusing on shape.

### ❯❯Discussing tone and experimenting with charcoal and chalk

The children could use charcoal and chalk for this project. It is an opportunity to revise the concepts

Mr Twit, marker pen drawing, Year 4

of tone and mark with them. Discuss the concept of tone with the children. For example, use a colour image on a television or video and reduce the colour until the same image is black and white. Ask the children to point out the darkest and lightest tones. Look at some black and white photographs. Ask the children to show you where the darkest tones are. Cut up some black and white photographs from a newspaper into small pieces and ask children to sort the fragments into dark medium and light tones. If you are sure they understand what you mean by 'tone' they can practice making their own tones with the charcoal and chalk. (See pages 64-69 'Teaching Art at Key Stage 1')

"Practice making a range of dark and light tones with the charcoal and chalk. Try using the charcoal and chalk in different ways. Try different methods of mixing the charcoal and chalk together. We will talk about the discoveries you make."

## ❚❚ Discussing mark and experimenting with making marks

Move on to discussing making marks. It is fun to demonstrate mark-making with the whole class. Arrange an easel in front of the children with a number of large sheets of paper on ready for some drawing. Ask the children for words that could describe how to make a mark. You could link this with talking about the experiments on texture and to the different surface qualities of the materials children may have explored through their science activities.

"Who could come up and make a mark as roughly as they can? Can any one come up and make an even rougher looking mark? Who can come up and make a mark that looks really soft and gentle? Be as soft and gentle as you can. Who can come out and make a mark that looks so sharp that it might cut your hand if you could grab it?

We have made marks that are rough, soft and sharp. What other words can you suggest that could go with a mark? Every time we choose a word one of you can come up to the easel and make a mark that might go with the word."

For example, the children might try: fast, slow, lazy, jagged, pitted, tangled etc.

Another way of doing this exercise would be to ask children to suggest anything that has an interesting surface. You could have collected some examples in advance: dry toast, very soft material,

Stig, Year 5

a bundle of thorns, rusted metal, feathers, putty. First ask the children to suggest words or phrases to describe the surfaces of the collection and then ask volunteers to attempt to make marks at the easel to go with the words that have been suggested. After working together it is important to let the children experiment on their own. (See pages 70-72 'Teaching Art at Key Stage 1')

"Now you can make a sheet of marks of your own. Try out some of the ideas we found together and then go on and invent new ways of making your own marks. Experiment as much as you like."

Materials and Resources:
Charcoal and chalk
Buff or off-white sugar paper
Large sheets of paper
An easel or flip chart
Marker pens
Drawing boards
Drawing media for the children's own experiments
Hair spray to fix the charcoal and chalk

### Talking about the characters of Mr and Mrs Twit

This project works the best if children are new to the novel. Read them extracts from the story that describe the characters of Mr and Mrs Twit Discuss the visual qualities of both Mr and Mrs Twit. Do not show the children the illustrations in the book at this stage. It is a richer activity if they come up with visual ideas themselves.

"If you could touch the beard of Mr Twit, what would it be like? What is his hair like. What about Mrs. Twit? What would her skin be like?"

### Drawing Mr and Mrs Twit

At this point the children could try some mark making experiments that explore different ways of showing Mr Twit's beard or Mrs Twit's hair. The problem here is that they will be itching just to draw Mr and Mrs Twit. A better strategy may be to focus on all the visual clues in the descriptions of the characters; you could make a list of relevant words or ask the children to listen to the descriptions again and remember them. For example, concentrate on all the bits of food caught up in Mr Twit's beard. The class could add in their own additional characterisations. Before the children start drawing remind them of the tone and mark experiments and talk about possible ways of using the charcoal and chalk to draw Mr and Mrs Twit.

"You are each going to have a large sheet of paper to make your own imaginary portrait drawing of Mr Twit. There is no need to draw all of him it may be best to just draw the top half of his body or even just his head and shoulders. Use both the charcoal and the chalk to give your drawing a range of tones. Remember how you can make light, dark or medium tones with the charcoal and chalk.

Most important is to remember that you can use the charcoal and chalk in many different ways to make different kinds of marks. You may want to experiment in your sketchbooks before you make your large drawing. Try out different ways of showing what you think Mr Twit's beard would be like if you could feel it. You have a large sheet of paper so think big! When you have finished Mr Twit collect a second sheet and draw Mrs Twit."

Materials and Resources:
Charcoal and chalk
Large sheets of paper
Drawing boards
Masking tape
Hair spray
Sketchbooks
Mr Twit by Roald Dahl

### Having an exhibition

If the children have been drawing on paper attached to the drawing boards by masking tape, it is easy to mount a quick exhibition. Prop the finished drawings up along the wall of the corridor or in the school hall. Ask the children to choose their favourite Mr and Mrs Twit. Ask them for reasons for their choice. Ask them who drew the most disgusting looking beard! Compare different styles of drawing - for example, some children will have been more careful about the details, others more original and daring in the way they drew Mr Twit's beard.

An issue here is the question what are the children looking for when they choose their favourite drawings? How do we choose what we like? The aim of this session is to help children to be more

Mrs Twit Year 4

careful and thoughtful about the judgments they make about what they think is a 'good' drawing. There is no reason why children cannot become aware of some of the values that underpin their individual taste for one style of work or another.

### Looking at the book illustrations

Make a connection to the illustrations in the book. These are small but it is possible to enlarge them on the photocopier. Ask the children to compare their own illustrations with those in the book. Which do they prefer? Why? Why are the illustrations in the book so small? How could they make their own drawings smaller?

### Working with a visiting graphic artist and book illustrator

The following sessions are examples of related work that could be generated if a graphic designer and book illustrator visited the school. The artist could help stimulate new work that builds extensively on ideas developed in this chapter. The children could invent their own characters for imaginative stories and develop their own illustrations. The new work could follow a similar

Looking at an artist's preparatory drawings for book illustrations

structure to the earlier sessions: talking about ideas, investigating and drawing. There is an opportunity to use sketchbooks to help children develop ideas and story boards before making finished illustrations.

### Planning an artist's visit to the school

There are a number of ways of providing opportunities for children to understand the ways artists work. Artists can work in the classroom with the children, visiting for one day or a number

Using sketchbooks to research ideas for illustrations from library books

of days each term. They can help develop new skills or bring fresh ideas to the children's work. Artists can help develop the art curriculum and support school-based art In-service training.

Projects might involve artists-in-residence over a period of time. Artists can also be employed by a school to work as artists making art, rather than as a kind of art teacher. One school employed an artist as part of its development plan. The artist was to bring their professional expertise into the school to help enhance the visual environment both inside and out in the playground.

Illustrations and storyboards, Year 6

Sometimes outside agencies will promote and support an artist working in school. The artist might combine two roles. First, time could be set aside for their own art practice. Second, they could work with the children in or outside the classroom. It might be possible to organise a visit to an artist's studio or workshop. A book called 'Artists in Schools', written by Caroline Sharp and Karen Dust and published by the National Foundation for Education Research in 1990, describes many of the issues and practical problems associated with inviting artists to work in your school.

For the project described in this chapter the artist was a graphic designer and book illustrator. He was also a parent. He visited for half a day to talk about how he worked and to show the children examples of his art.

The previous sessions in this chapter form examples of a unit of work designed to help

children illustrate a character from a story. A visit by a book illustrator could be linked to such work and become a central part of the planning for art that term. The project should also form part of the language curriculum. There are many other kinds of artist who may be invited to visit the class: painters, sculptors, fabric designers, architects, photographers, graphic designers, landscape architects to name but a few examples.

## Talking to a graphic designer and book illustrator

The artist explained to the children the processes involved in illustration. This included reading the manuscript, using a sketchbook to research ideas, making roughs and storyboards, making preliminary drawings and sketches on tracing paper and then developing the final art work. For example, the designer explained how he used a special textured paper for water colour. He explained how the particular texture of the paper affected the look of the drawing. The class teacher was able to reinforce the idea that the choice of materials affects the look of the finished product. The children discussed the advantages and disadvantages of using charcoal, HB pencils and paint for an illustration. The children looked through a portfolio of the artists work and were given enough time to ask lots of questions.

## Identifying stories or books to illustrate and making story boards

The teacher and the artist helped the children discover that there are different types of illustrations appropriate to different kinds of book. In the library the children discovered illustrations for bible stories, cartoons, imaginative stories, history books, geography books and other reference books. They discussed possible stories or books might be good to use as starting points for their own illustrations.

## Researching ideas in the sketchbooks

Using the artist's own examples of storyboards as a stimulus the children experimented with story boards for their chosen books. The children used sketchbooks to collect visual material that might be useful. For example, if a drawing of a castle was appropriate for a story then the child was encouraged to use the library to find illustrations or photographs of different castles. A useful illustration or photograph could be copied. Any source of visual material might be used to help develop an illustration.

Illustration for an imaginative story, Year 3 (see next page)

## )))Children draw their own illustration for a story or book

The children were asked to select one panel from their storyboards to develop into an illustration. The children also selected a short passage of text relevant to the illustration that might need to be included later as part of the page. The artist showed the children a specific water colour technique. The artist was able to help children with this new way of painting.

Having drawn and painted an illustration and linked this to a passage of text, the children used their sketch books again to design a layout for the text and illustration on the page (a computer is also a valuable tool for this task).

The children could go on to write their own story which they might then illustrate. The teacher could find some appropriate text. Each child could have one paragraph or page to illustrate. These could be combined later in a class book. This class would be well equipped to progress onto writing, designing, illustrating and producing a newspaper or magazine of their own.

The artist's visit was important in highlighting the value of sketchbook and investigative work. The children saw how much work goes into developing visual ideas. The artist worked on projects over a period of time and was used to leaving work unfinished to return to at a later date. The artist explained how he had been trained and that now he had his own business, he was self-employed as a graphic designer and book illustrator. The teacher used the process that the artist described as a model upon which the children's own book illustration project was based.

### Materials and Resources:
Pencils
Water colours and brushes
Cartridge paper
Sketchbooks
Drawing and writing media

Pattern for fabric printed with polystyrene tiles, Year 4 (see page 36)

# Pattern, different cultures and IT

## ❙❙❙ Talking about patterns

"Who is wearing a pattern? Can you show us? Who is wearing a pattern of lines? Who is wearing a pattern of shapes? Who is wearing a pattern of colours? What is the difference between a pattern and a picture? A pattern must have something that repeats itself a number of times. What can you see in the classroom that has parts that repeat again and again? Where can you see patterns in the classroom?"

Simple exercises and starting points for projects on pattern can be found in 'Teaching Art at Key Stage 1' pages 26-35.

## ❙❙❙ Collecting patterns from home

Ask the children to bring in from home something that has a pattern. Talk about the possibilities: fabric off-cuts, wallpaper, items of clothing, bags and boxes, food packaging, things from the kitchen. Make a display with the collected objects. Enhance the collection with patterns found in school. Has the local fabric shop, carpet shop or DIY store got any old pattern books to give or lend? For example, the Laura Ashley catalogue provides an example of contemporary British domestic interior design that uses a great many patterns on different materials and coverings.

Making patterns with natural materials

## ❙❙❙ Collecting patterns in sketchbooks

Ask the children to collect some examples of the patterns in their sketch books. Remind them that there is no need to draw all of the object. They only need to draw enough of the pattern in order to show clearly it is a pattern. The children could use a view finder (a small window cut in a sheet of paper or card) to isolate small areas of pattern.

Materials and Resources:
Sketchbooks
Drawing media
View finder

## ❙❙❙ Making a collection of natural patterns

As a contrast to the preceding exercise, make a collection of natural patterns. Magnifying glasses and a microscope may be useful. Many natural patterns can be photocopied from illustrations and photographs in books. Enlarge the patterns for a

Talking about patterns

display, or use the photocopies as material that the children can select and collect in small sketchbook collages. The children can continue by drawing the natural patterns. Patterns can also be collected by making rubbings.

Materials and Resources:
Sketchbooks
Drawing media
Collection of natural patterns
Magnifying glasses and a microscope
Camera
Photocopier

## Making a large scale drawing from a small scale pattern

This is a good exercise to help the children with ideas about scale as well as giving them the confidence to think big.

"First draw a small box about five centimetres square in your sketchbooks. Find a small pattern, use the magnifying glass. Some of you may be able to use a microscope. When you have chosen a pattern make a drawing of it in the box. Make sure you fill the box right to the edges.

Here are some very large sheets of paper. On each sheet is a box half a metre square. Here are some marker pens. Draw your pattern really large in the big boxes. You will have to think big. To help, look carefully at the shapes, the lines and the marks that make up the small pattern you drew first."

Materials and Resources:
Sketchbooks
Drawing media
A1 sheets
Something large and flat to rest on
Marker pens
The collection of made and natural patterns

## Researching patterns from a different culture

Ask the children's parents if they can bring in any patterns that are special to their culture, religion or country of origin. Are there any fabrics or items of clothing that can be borrowed? Are there any photographs or books that can be used in a display? If you visit local places of worship you may be able to find some examples of patterns that are linked in some way with a specific religion or cultural identity.

The school library may also be a rich source of patterns from many different parts of the world. Ask the children to see what they can find.

The Pitt Rivers Museum in Oxford and the Museum of Mankind in London are excellent

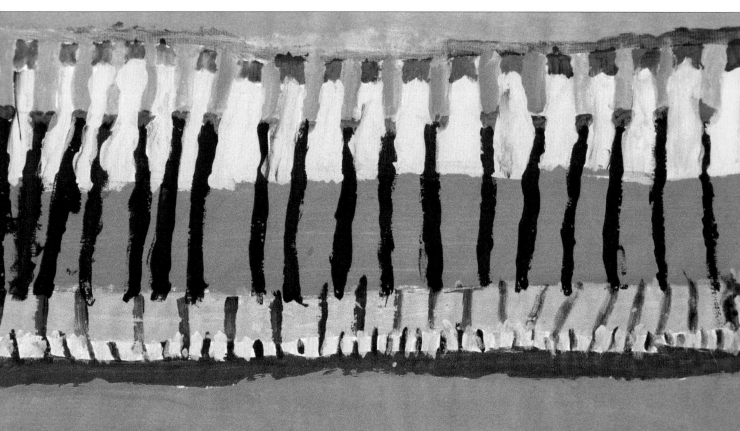

A pattern design, Year 4 using paint rather than marker pens

Patterns from Ecuador (from: 'Indian Designs from Ancient Ecuador', F.W. Shaffer)

sources for many different patterns collected, some might argue plundered, from numerous different cultures. It is possible to buy many cheaply priced postcards and books that could provide reources for projects such as this for many years. Try your local museum, perhaps their curator or education officer may help.

One of the delights of this work is the possible richness and variety of pattern making. A sumptuous and exciting display of pattern will feed the children's own art for many weeks.

### ▌▌▌Collecting examples of patterns from different parts of the world

Ask the children to use their sketchbooks to make their own collection of patterns from other cultures. A view finder might help the children focus on a part of a pattern: there is no need to draw the whole of a patterned object or image. Again, they may wish to draw or make collages from photocopied material. An instamatic camera may be useful.

Exciting work is possible with a video disk camera linked to a computer printer. It may be increasingly possible to find many examples of patterns in CD ROM collections. If your school has access to scanning facilities, try scanning patterns onto a disk. The children can then explore the possibilities

of colouring, cutting, pasting, moving and printing the stored patterns.

**Materials and Resources:**
Sketchbooks
Drawing media
View finder
Camera
Photocopier
A display or collection of patterns
IT, including possibilities for video disk cameras, scanned patterns, CD ROM collections

### ▌▌Designing a pattern

"Out of all the patterns you have seen, which is your favourite? Choose a part of that pattern, a shape for example, or perhaps a line. Use the shape or line as part of a new pattern of your own. Think up some ideas and try them out in your sketchbook first. When you are sure you know what you would like the design of your pattern to look like, use the small A6 pieces of paper and draw your pattern out to fill the whole sheet. Make sure the pattern goes right up to all four sides of the paper. Use colour as well."

A more prescriptive but also more focused approach would be to limit the children to using motifs from one culture. This would mean that their own pattern had the character of, say, an Islamic or Celtic pattern.

**Materials and Resources:**
Sketchbooks
Drawing media
A6 paper

A collection of patterns, prints and applied designs, Year 3

## ❚❚Applying the pattern design

Try a number of ideas:
The children could use their pattern to decorate a plate. Use paper plates. An even better idea is to use a mould technique. For example, use an enamel or hard plastic plate or bowl as a base and cover over the plate with a film of margarine. Then apply three layers of torn tissue paper coated in wallpaper or cold water starch paste. The margarine will allow the hardened tissue paper to be easily removed from the plate when it dries. The children can choose different colours. While the paste is wet add a final layer of tissue. The wallpaper paste will allow the children to smooth the tissue onto the form of the plate or bowl. This final layer can be a pattern of colours and shapes. The children could also add a variety of different media and materials to create a pattern. They might use string, metallic papers, wool, thin fabric shapes, coloured shapes or fragments of paper that they have decorated with a pattern of their own (see page 33).

Buy a paper linen effect table cloth from a supermarket. Use large felt pens to draw out one design or perhaps a number of the children's individual designs. Children will need to think big. Use strips of white fabric so that the children can apply their patterns to make headbands, scarves or ties. Use fabric crayons or paints.

Remind the children how to print using polystyrene tiles. Ask them to transfer their pattern to a tile and then print the design. They

Decorated plate, Year 3

Large fabric designs on paper tablecloth, Year 3

Printing patterns using polystyrene tiles, Year 3

could use their pattern as a motif for a greetings card or gift wrapping paper.

Ask the children to suggest other things that might be decorated with their pattern. Whether the children go on to work on plates, fabric or make prints the key to this unit of work is the successful application of a design. The complication for primary school children is that the process and media used affect the way a pattern can be applied. Shapes cut from tissue paper may not be the best way of making a complex pattern inspired by Celtic knots. Older Juniors, in Year 5 and 6, might be challenged to design a pattern appropriate to the process that they will be using to make or decorate their artefact. Equally, they may be challenged to devise a process appropriate to a pattern they had previously designed.

## ❚❚ Design possibilities using a computer

It is just as important that children can investigate and develop ideas for computer generated designs - in fact it is vital as it is all too easy to generate facile and rather crude patterns using a computer. Look back at the previous sessions in this chapter. Children used a variety of patterned source material to generate their own designs. Other

Painted fabric, Year 3

ideas for source material that might inspire new computer-aided designing include: geometric designs found in architecture, woven textiles, bead work, masks, and ceramic decoration from a variety of countries and cultures.

Areas of a drawn picture or shape can be filled with colour and the colour combinations changed at will. Geometric shapes such as squares, rectangles and triangles can be manipulated by reflection on screen. Images can be enlarged and reduced in size.

Images can be edited, altered and worked without damaging the original. Encourage children to regularly save their design. Each class project could be allocated a separate disk. This disk will include all the individual designs from one project.

Many programmes have other facilities. The children can explore different ways of manipulating an image on the screen. They can reposition images and then repeat small areas of a pattern or motif all over the screen. This links well to designs for wallpaper, wrapping paper and printed textiles.

Use any draw or paint software package. The tools include the option to draw freehand and geometrically using a range of brush sizes and colours. Children can work with existing images that are scanned. Computer generated images can be used for many purposes - remember that the computer is an essentiall tool in contemporary graphic design.

## Transferring images from computer to fabric

As an example of how technology can be applied to a design project, the photographs show work that resulted from a technique for transferring designs from the computer to fabric.

Change the normal print cartridge or ribbon for one designed specially for use with fabric. These cartridges contain a special ink which will transfer the printed image from paper to fabric by ironing.

The children can explore the effect of how the same printed paper image can be used several times. Each time the image is ironed onto a new piece of fabric it lightens in colour.

Why not use this process to print designs on T-shirts? This could become part of a mini-enterprise project. The materials and blank T-shirts can be costed. The products are original designs and could be sold to family and friends.
There is a newer method that involves the use of

Images transferred from computer to fabric, Year6

specialised paper rather than a different ink cartridge, This is expensive but is easier in that there is no need to change the printer's cartridge each time you print. You will be able to find out more about such products from an IT equipment suppliers catalogue.

## Working in black and white without using special ink or paper

You can buy a commercial product which can be brushed onto any black and white image. The image can then be iron transferred onto fabric and the children can use fabric crayons, paints or pens to add their own colour scheme.

As an alternative to the commercial product you can make your own mixture. Use equal quantities of water and white spirit with a drop of washing up liquid. For safety reasons the teacher should make this mixture in advance.

Materials and Resources:
Computer
Software
Sublimatic ink cartridge or specialist paper that allows the iron transfer of images to fabric
A mixture of water and white spirit
Washing-up liquid

One group suggested using the colour printouts to make jewellery. The colour printouts were glued onto thin card and the children cut the card into many different shapes. The children used a hole punch and threaded these shapes onto coloured raffia to make wrist bands, anklets and necklaces. Other children made earrings or brooches. One child remembered that the school had a laminator and asked if was practical to laminate her cardboard shapes. Another boy worked out that he could use PVA to give his patterned jewellery a glossy finish.

Materials and Resources:
Computer print outs of designs
Card
PVA
Scissors
Hole punch
Raffia

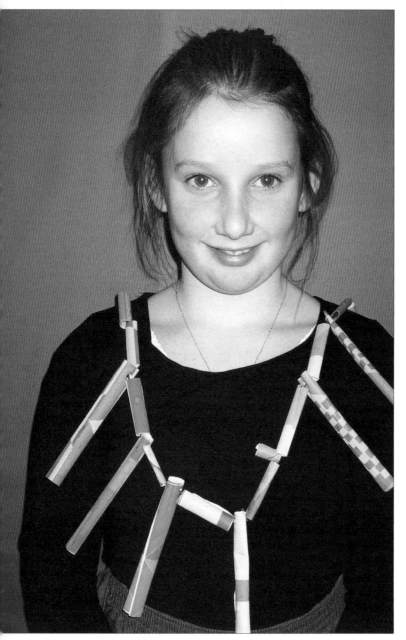

Jewellery made from colour printouts

## ◗ Other uses for colour printouts

"You have designed patterns using the computer. Can you think up other ways of using the print outs of your patterns? Work in groups to 'brainstorm' a number of ideas. Don't forget to think about what tools or materials you will need. We will share the ideas you develop and talk about the practical problems involved in trying them out."

Jungle collage detail, Year 3 (see page 45)

## An indoor jungle

Collect together different houseplants from around the school. It is best to have a number of different sized plants that have different kinds of leaves. The more plants that can be collected together, the larger and more exciting will be the indoor jungle that you can create in the classroom. You could make the jungle in the centre of the room with plants covering the top of a circular table. Try placing plants on the floor both underneath and around the table. The effect is of a confusion of different plants. After the initial set of activities the indoor jungle can be moved to make a display at the side of the classroom.

**Materials and Resources:**
Houseplants

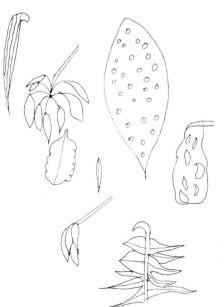

Leaf-shapes from sketchbook, Year 3

## Focusing on shape

The first exercise is one of the warm up and revision exercises designed to help the children focus on one of the visual elements, in this case shape. Refer to page 79 where an introduction to shape is described in full. If the children have not worked in this way before, or if this basic work on shape needs revising, start this project with a version of the work described on page 79. Even if the children are experienced young artists it is still worth devising a simple warm-up exercise to help them re-focus on the relevant visual element.

If you give the children drawing media such as biros, fibre-tipped pens or black wax crayons they will not be able to rub out their shape drawings. Look at pages 53-54 for a discussion about how to build the children's confidence to draw without worrying too much about making mistakes.

## Collecting leaf shapes from the indoor jungle

Collecting leaf shapes from the indoor jungle

Now the children will find it very easy to move on to collecting all the different leaf shapes they can find in the indoor jungle.

"Look at the leaves in the indoor jungle. What are some of the differences between the shapes of the leaves? Look at this leaf. How would you describe its shape? Here is another leaf that looks completely different to the first one. What happens when you look at the same leaf from different angles? What words would you use to describe its shape?

Use your sketchbooks to collect the different shapes of the leaves in the indoor jungle. Try to show the special shape that each leaf has. Even leaves from the same plant may have very different shapes. Try to show that the leaf shapes have different sizes, some may look quite large on the page, others may be very small. But don't make all your drawings too tiny! The shape of a leaf will change depending on your view point. Try drawing the same leaf from different positions. There is no need to put in all the detail you can see on each leaf."

It is not necessary to be too strict about drawing in detail, some children will enjoy showing all the veins and patterns visible in each leaf but they should be collecting a number of different examples and not spending too much time on one drawing. You may need to emphasise that the children should draw only the leaves not the whole plant. You could easily extend this exercise by asking the children to collect examples of leaf shapes from the environment around the school.

Materials and resources:
Drawing media
Sketchbooks
The indoor jungle of houseplants

Looking at Rousseau's painting 'Surprised, Storm in the Forest'

## Talking about Rousseau's painting 'Surprised, Storm in the Forest'

You could start this jungle project by discussing this painting first. You could use any painting or drawing that shows a variety of leaves. Another option would be show the children fabrics that are designed with a leaf motif. This latter choice would be particularly appropriate if you were thinking of fabric designs as one of the possible outcomes for the project.

The children can be asked to list everything they can see in the painting. They could then discuss the different shapes of all the leaves that Rousseau had painted and the shapes of some of the other components of the image, particularly the shape of the tiger including its teeth and tail. The foliage shows a variety of different greens. Children can comment on the differences in the colour used to show the leaves. You could go on to ask the class what they thought was happening in the painting? What was the tiger doing? What was the tiger feeling? How would they feel if they were in the painting? What was going to happen next? The teacher might ask the children about their opinions of Rousseau's painting. What did they like about it? What did they dislike? Would they put the painting up at home to look at every day? If not, why not?

Materials and Resources:
Rousseau's painting 'Surprised, Storm in the Forest' or another jungle or forest painting, an alternative is a collection of fabrics with flora and fauna motifs

## Practical activities following the discussion

The children could use sketchbooks to collect different examples of leaf shapes from Rousseau's painting. They could try mixing the variety of different greens that Rousseau used.

Materials and Resources:
Sketchbooks and drawing media
Soft pastels to mix a range of greens
Or all the equipment for mixing colours in paint (see pages 55-56)

## Investigating rain forest animals and making a collection of animal shapes in the sketchbooks

Make a library search and collect together in the classroom or library area books that include illustrations of animals that live in the rain forest.

"Use your sketch books and make some simple drawings to show the different shapes of some of the

Imaginative jungle drawing, Year 3

animals that live in rain forests and jungles. Can you tell what kind of animal you were looking at from the shape you have drawn?"

All the advice about work on drawing shapes on page 79 can be repeated here. It is possible to organise different groups to collect different categories of animals or perhaps make sure that each group has to include at least one bird, insect, mammal, reptile etc. Children can gain confidence if they are allowed to trace the animal shape first. Ask them to practice drawing the same animal freehand immediately after tracing its shape. This will help the children's confidence to draw.

Materials and Resources:
Sketchbooks and drawing media
Tracing paper
A collection of books with photographs or illustrations of rainforest animals

## Making imaginative or observational jungle drawings

An alternative at this stage would be to ask children to make a straightforward observational drawing of the indoor jungle. You could set the children up to draw with drawing boards and large sheets of paper. Ask them to focus on shape. They could use a view finder to help focus on a section of the indoor jungle (look at page 31 for advice on

using view finders). Pages 47-54 give detailed advice about drawing projects that you could adapt for this jungle work.

It might be more appropriate for the class to use their initial investigations and the stimulus of the houseplant collection to make an imaginative rather than a strictly observed response.

"You are going to use the drawing boards and some large sheets of paper to make a rain forest drawing of your own. You will need to be able to see our indoor jungle whilst you work but you do not need to copy it exactly. You will need your sketchbooks beside you. You can look at the sketchbooks and use ideas from

Leaves from sketchbook, Year 3

Imaginative jungle drawing, Year 3

them whenever you like. You can make your jungle drawing in any way you choose but here are a few things I would like you to think about:

Draw lots of different kinds of leaves, give them different shapes and sizes. The leaves in our indoor jungle and in Rousseau's painting overlap one on top of another. You should draw your jungle leaves overlapping or covering each other."

The children may need help to grasp the practical implications of the concept of overlapping. If this is the case it may be appropriate to design an activity that allows the class to experiment with overlapping shapes. For example, ask children to collect different leaf shapes, only instead of drawing each leaf separately on the page ask them to draw the shape of each new leaf overlapping one they have already collected.

"Start in the middle of your paper with leaves and work slowly towards the sides, the top and the bottom of the paper. You are using a fibre-tipped pen or black wax crayon so you can't rub out bits you don't like. So there is no point worrying about

mistakes, everybody will make them, just keep going.

Draw lots of the jungle before you start putting in any animals. You can look at our indoor jungle and copy the leaves if you find that helpful. Don't draw the pots. There are no plant pots in a real jungle.

Look at some of the books from the library again if there are any other animals that you didn't collect in your sketchbooks first time around. You can look at Rousseau's painting for ideas, but do not copy the painting - this is a jungle drawing of your own."

This work is not in colour - the line drawings can be very graphic and exciting without adding colour. However colour could easily become a feature of the project not only through work on greens but also looking at the exotic colours of some jungle birds and animals.

Primary school children do not find it easy to visualise how to compose a drawing that will fit the space of the paper. For example, some children will make very small drawings, others will draw along a narrow strip at the bottom of the paper. In this project the advice to start in the middle of the paper and the further suggestion that the drawing could spread out from the centre towards the edges will help. Children will feel more confident about where to start, they are therefore more likely to draw fluently, naturally filling the paper with their drawing. However, this is only one compositional device and there are many other ways to set about composing a drawing. The point of using this approach here is to simplify the problem of composition for the children as they have already more than enough to think about as they concentrate on shapes, overlapping and so on.

## Talking about the finished drawings

The children will learn a lot by looking at each others work and by being asked to comment on what they like and admire. Leave the drawings fixed to the drawing boards and have an exhibition, propping the boards up along a wall.

Materials and resources:
Drawing boards
Paper
Drawing media
Masking tape or clips
The indoor jungle
Rousseau's painting or other examples of art, craft and design with a forest or jungle feel
The children's sketchbooks

## Developing the jungle project - making a paper collage

There are many ways teachers could develop this jungle idea. For example, the basic investigative and imaginative work could inform work in clay, paint, collage, printing, design, and sculptural construction. On page 45 is an example of collage work that could be developed from the work done so far. Collage naturally involves possibilities for overlapping shapes, a theme that emerged in the earlier drawing sessions.

Apart from the jungle theme this technique for making a paper collage can be adapted to work for many different themes, topics or starting points. This process was also described for infants on pages 24 and 25, 'Teaching Art at Key Stage 1'.

## Using relevant examples of art and design

The Year 3 class that completed the work illustrated, visited the huge panels by the artist Frank Brangwyn that fill the walls of the Brangwyn Hall in Swansea. These panels feature Brangwyn's treatment of the richness of flora and fauna from countries that formed the old British Empire. The

Studying the Brangwyn Panels in Swansea

children drew parts of the panels in their sketchbooks and discussed the differences between Brangwyn's work and what they had achieved. A visit to make observational drawings in a tropical planthouse or greenhouse also could become an important part of this project.

The children also looked at extracts from Walt Disney's 'Jungle Book' and it might be possible to use other short video extracts from films that feature the rain forest. Looking at Disney's film could become the start of a different project that builds on the work to involve drawing and cutting out animal and plant shapes. If the work is extended in this way, look at ways of making legs, heads and tails move. The children could then animate a two dimensional jungle scene by using a video camera with an animation facility.

The children could work on more ornamental designs for the collages. There are many fabric designs that have tropical or exotic plants as an underlying theme. Find some examples to show the children. The is no doubt that the specific

examples of relevant art and design that you discuss with the class will deeply effect decisions they make in their own work.

## ⦀Colouring sugar papers

Coloured sugar paper is often available in school. However the colours are not very exciting. Jungles are rich in colour, particularly a rich variety of greens. This first process is designed to enable children to create their own coloured papers for use in the collage.

The children will need plenty of different coloured sugar paper for the collage. Ask them to use soft pastels and experiment with different ways of applying new colour to the paper.

"Can you think up different ways of using the pastels? How about using the side, pressing hard or pressing softly? Can you think up ways of making marks to make a patterned effects? How many different colours could you use? We could add at least two new colours to the sugar paper. What happens when you put one colour on top of another? Are there other ways you could combine the colours? There will be many different ways that you could colour the paper."

For a jungle collage you could ask the children to make many sheets of different greens. This task can be linked to the investigation of the different greens they discovered in the leaves of the house plants or to an exploration of greens in the landscape prior to making a landscape drawing or painting (see pages 49). Jungle flowers, fruits, birds and animals will need a different range of colours. There is great potential here for rich and varied mark and pattern making.

The sheets of coloured papers will need to be sprayed with hair spray to prevent too much dust and smudging before the children move on to the next stage. There are other possibilities for making a resource bank of different coloured papers for use in a collage. Try using other materials and techniques to colour the papers. For example, more confident children could be given a choice of pastels, paint, inks, marbling equipment and diffusion sprays, in fact this session could have a strong focus on experimenting with how different materials create different effects.

Concentrating on cutting leaf shapes

Materials and resources:
Lots of small sheets (A4 seemed a good size) of different coloured sugar paper
Soft pastels, you can use coloured chalks but the pastels have strong colours (the project will work with many different methods of colouring the paper, the children could use paint, inks, marbling techniques for example)
A box to store the coloured sheets and a waste bag or box
Polythene to cover the tables, this session is messy!

Jungle collage, Year 3

## ◗◗ Tearing and cutting leaf shapes

"You can use scissors or tear the leaf shapes. Look at the pages in your sketchbooks where you collected all the different leaf shapes. Look at all the different leaves in our indoor jungle. Look at the leaf shapes in Rousseau's painting. Remember how different one shape is from another. You said that some are large, some are small, some are pointed, some are rounded, some are thin, some shapes are repeated again and again and some are complicated. So remember to make a variety of different shapes and sizes of leaves. As you work store the finished leaf shapes carefully."

Materials and Resources:
Pre-coloured sheets of paper
Scissors
Somewhere to store all the paper leaves.

## ◗ Making the collage

In our project the children worked in groups and pooled the coloured papers and then the leaf shapes. Each group made one panel of a large class collage. However, children could work on individual collages or perhaps the whole class could become involved in making one shared end product..

## ◗ Adding animals and flowers

The children will want to add animals to the collage. They may also want to add other things such as fruits, flowers, even jungle people. The collage may be entirely imaginary. To prepare for this follow the steps from the heading 'Colouring sugar papers' only allow for the different colours and shapes needed for animals and so on. Some children may find it easier to draw the animal shapes on the reverse side of the coloured paper and cut these drawn shapes out with scissors.

Children may find it helpful to be allowed to trace the shapes of animals and then transfer the traced images to the back of the coloured sugar paper. After all a designer would not hesitate to use computer technology to copy relevant animal shapes. The children could make cardboard stencils which will be useful for drawing around to

Practising glueing paper shapes

repeat the same shape many times. Look back at page 41 for ideas to help children collect and record different animal shapes. There are aesthetic choices to be made here. Older and more advanced children will have the knowledge and experience needed to make informed judgements about the approach they wish to adopt. If you can show children that there are a number of different possibilities they will take creative control over the work. In practice this has to be balanced with the pressure of the often limited time available for art and the need to ensure effective and workable classroom management.

## Composing the collage and starting to glue

If the children want their animals peering out from behind leaves they will need to plan for this before they glue too much down.

"There are many ways that you could arrange your shapes on the paper to compose the collage. Where would you like to start on the paper? Is it best to start with small leaves or larger leaves? How will the animals fit in? What will you need to do if you have too many shapes for the size of paper? Can your collage have too much in it? Choose some of the shapes you like and start arranging them on this large sheet of paper, don't forget the shapes can overlap. When you are satisfied begin to glue the shapes carefully on the paper. Remember this system to help you glue without getting in a mess:

Your working area is divided into two with a strip of masking tape.

Keep a clean side of the area for your collage.

The glue spreader, glue, sponges for sticky fingers and newspaper always stay on the dirty side of the area.

Always glue on a clean sheet of newspaper, so put a new sheet of newspaper down on the gluing side of the area every time you glue a new shape. If you have an old magazine to glue on, turn a page each time you glue a new shape, then you won't get glue on everything. Don't use too much glue, if it squeezes out from underneath the paper when you press the shape down on the collage you have used too much.

Glue over the edges so that the paper shapes stick flat. Use the sponges to wipe glue off your fingers and any small drops that fall on the collage or the table.

If you are working as a group why not organise yourselves into a team so that different children have different jobs to do?"

Some groups will find the task of arranging the shapes for their collage and then gluing down the leaves difficult since it is the leaf shapes nearest the paper that need to be glued down first. This means that the arrangement will need to be disturbed before it can be glued down permanently.

**Materials and Resources:**
Polythene to cover tables
Masking tape to mark out clean and dirty areas
PVA
Glue containers
Glue spreaders
Slightly damp sponges or rags
Scissors
Coloured paper shapes to make the collage with

## Displaying the jungle collages

Each group of children can make a panel for a large jungle scene that fills one wall of the classroom. The jungle may look better if the class uses a consistent colour as a background for the collage. The Year 3 children who made the collages illustrated in this chapter thought that the coloured leaves and animals looked best glued onto black paper.

# Landscape drawings and paintings

Landscape drawing, shape, tone and texture, Year 6 (see page 53)

## Starting points

The following paragraphs contain ideas about starting work on landscape. The idea is to choose one (or more) of the visual elements as a focus for the landscape drawing and painting. This approach may be adapted to work with almost any theme, topic or initial stimulus. If the children have recently worked with an appropriate visual element (for example they have may have been working with shape for the preceding jungle project in chapter two), there will be no need to repeat some of the basic experimental work. However it is too easy to undervalue the effect of simple warm-up exercises. Try to find some way of allowing the children to explore, experiment and investigate before expecting them to produce finished art work. If the children have worked from the landscape before, choose a new starting point which focuses on a visual element that suggests a different way of looking at the subject.

### ▌▌Starting with shape

Look at the work described on page 79. This could be used as a basis to prepare children before they begin drawing a landscape. Ask the children to use their sketchbooks to collect some of the different shapes they can see in the landscape. The shapes of fields, trees, bushes, houses, clouds, hills, pylons, factories, sheds, cranes. This works well for rural, semi-rural, urban or industrial landscapes.

**Materials and Resources:**
Sketchbooks and drawing media

Collecting shapes from a landscape

Exploring colour in the landscape

## ❚❚ Starting with colour, using pastels

If the children worked through the rain forest project they may well have investigated mixing a range of greens with the soft pastels, see page 44. Exploring different greens is a useful starting point for landscape work in pastel. If they have already experimented with different greens, why not take the children outside with their sketchbooks and ask them to explore some of the other colours that make up the landscape? If they are experimenting, remind them that there is no need to draw pictures, patches of colour are fine: it is

Exploring greens, Year 4

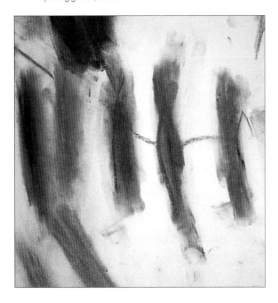

only the colours that are important. The idea here is that the children should attempt to mix the kinds of colours they can see. This can be a difficult task. To help, give the children two chances to find appropriate colours. First, encourage them to experiment without worrying about making the colours too accurate. They will find many appropriate colours by accident. Second time

around, ask the children to be more careful about recording only colours that they can find in the landscape. Ask children to think of ways of describing or naming the colours they have created and observed.

Materials and Resources:
Sketchbooks
Pastels
Hair spray to fix the experiments

## ❚❚ Starting with colour, using paint

The same ideas could be approached using paint. Colour mixing is a basic skill that children should have learnt and practised at Key Stage 1. (For advice about teaching children a colour mixing technique, see pages 39-41 of 'Teaching Art at Key Stage 1'.) A summary of the technique can be found on page 55. In good weather it is possible for children to take the equipment they need and paint outside; or they could use paint to recreate some of the landscape colours they discovered using the sketchbooks and pastels. This work is still experimental and the children should not be trying to paint pictures. They could simply make a lot of patches of colour on white paper.

## ❚❚ Other ways of exploring colour

Children could search for landscape colours in colour supplements and magazines. They could cut out fragments of colour and collage colour collections into their sketchbooks. The children might continue by matching some of the colours they found with paint they mixed for themselves.

Teachers may wish to link this work with simple colour theory. Are the children familiar with the colour wheel? Children should already know about primary and secondary colours. Do the children know how to make browns, tertiary colours? Children may be taught about complementary colours, opposites on a simple colour wheel, or the difference between hue and tone. Hue is the name we give to pigments, for example, the difference between say red and blue; a turquoise is a blue with a hue that tends towards green. Tone is lightness or darkness; a colour can tend towards white or black. Teachers may wish to introduce children to ideas about colour contrasts, colour harmonies and colour intensity. Children could experiment with colours that are warm or cold, neutral or with colour combinations that are discordant. It may be worth pointing out that commercial colour printing can use a different system; the colours cyan, magenta and yellow become their three 'primary colours'; printers use black to give greater intensity to dark colours.

The danger about imposing a too theoretical approach is that children will loose some of the spontaneity and enjoyment of simply mixing colours and making discoveries for themselves. It is certainly true that beautiful paintings can be made by children who have never seen a colour wheel and do not know what a complementary colour is. Some artists and teachers would argue that the children will make better paintings if they are not introduced to the theory too soon. Discovering and experimenting with colours is the key here whether or not colour theory is formally introduced.

Materials and Resources:
All the equipment needed for colour mixing (see pages 55-56 )
Colour supplements
PVA
Glue spreaders
A colour wheel
Information about colour theory

## Starting with tone

Give the children different drawing media, for example, charcoal and chalk, a range of graded pencils, black wax crayons, graphite and felt pens. Ask them to experiment in their sketchbooks - or on larger sheets of paper for a more dramatic effect. (See the chapter on tone in 'Teaching Art at Key Stage 1' pages 64-69.)

"Try and make the darkest patches of tone that you can and then patches that are the lightest or palest possible. Try and make a range of tones that vary from light to dark. Remember you are experimenting, trying to find out how these different drawing media can be used make light, dark and medium tones. There is no need to draw pictures."

This approach mirrors that used on pages 24 and 63. The children could also experiment with black and white paint or light and dark greens. Now take the class to look at the landscape you intend to draw or paint and talk about light and dark. It can be useful to link work in tone with the topic 'light' in science.

"Where can you see the darkest tones in this landscape? Where are the deepest shadows? Can you see any areas that are really light? Can you see any sunlight? If you half squint your eyes you can see less detail but the differences between light and dark tones stand out."

Materials and Resources:
Sketchbooks
Larger sheets of paper
Off white or buff sugar paper
A range of drawing media including different graded drawing pencils
The equipment needed for colour mixing ( see pages 55-56)

Drawing the foregound, Year 5

## Starting with space

Talk with the children about what they can see in the foreground, middleground and background. You could ask them to make lists. Explain how things look smaller as they get further away. Ask them to comment on examples in the landscape where trees, houses and so forth can look tiny in the distance. (Some simple strategies for introducing ideas about space to children are included in 'Teaching Art at Key Stage 1', see pages 59-63.)

"Here are three strips of paper. On the first strip draw everything that you can see way in the distance, think about the horizon line. On the second strip draw all the things that are close to us, all the things in the foreground. On the third piece of paper draw a strip of the middleground showing some of the things that are midway between where we are now and the horizon. These are practice drawings so don't worry about making mistakes and drawing too accurately but try and show as much of the foreground, middleground and background as you can."

Materials and Resources:
Sketchbooks and drawing media
Strips of paper

## Starting with line

Ask each of the children to contribute a line of their own to a large sheet of paper. Discuss words or phrases that might be used to describe these lines. Encourage the children to think up new and unusual ways of drawing lines.

"Now use your sketchbooks to collect some examples of different lines that you can find by searching around the classroom. There is no need to draw all of the objects you are looking at, just the lines you think are interesting."

I am always amazed by the inquisitiveness of children who will find lines in the most unusual places. This may lead to very inventive drawings.

"Now look at the landscape and collect some of the lines you can see. Look out for the horizon line, lines of hedges, roof lines, roads and paths, telephone lines, lines made by trees or clouds... Remember not to draw a picture, just collect lines."

Materials and Resources:
Sketchbooks and drawing media
A large sheet of paper on an easel for the initial class line collection

## Starting with pattern

Use the same approach suggested above but substitute pattern for line.

Exploring line in the playground with string and chalk

## Starting with texture

Work on texture and landscape should be preceded by explorations of mark making (see page 25).

"If you could touch the tree tops how do you think they would feel, what would the sky feel like if you could touch it? How about the clouds. Imagine you could reach out and feel the mountain side. What would that be like? Experiment in the sketchbooks by trying to invent some marks that show how parts of the landscape might feel if you could reach out and touch them. Remember not to draw a picture. You can use some of the ideas you discover to help you make your own landscape picture later."

An aim of this approach is to encourage children to use a variety of marks when they draw. They will then be able to find their own way of representing a mass of leaves from a group of trees or the faint wispy nature of high cloud.

Talking about texture

However, drawing the texture of cloud is a difficult concept to grasp. A better approach might be to focus on the marks that artists use to represent clouds or trees. Children could look at a selection of relevant paintings and drawings and use their sketchbooks to mimic the way different artists have used marks to show tactile qualities.

Materials and Resources:
Sketchbooks and
Drawing media

## Using these starting points

The starting points for landscape drawing mentioned here focus on the visual elements. For younger children, or children who have not had much experience of art, it is usually demanding enough to concentrate on one of the visual elements at a time. For older or more able children you could combine the tasks above into more complicated exercises. Try shapes that have tones, or colours that have shape and tone, or space shown only by using outline shapes - the variations are endless. The division of the visual elements is a device that helps us break down visual perception. In reality these visual elements work together and are irreducable to one quality alone. As children become more familiar with the mechanics of rendering colour, tone, shape and so on, it will become more and more natural for

them to combine these elements in their work. This experimental and investigative work is also a useful tool for developing descriptive language as it opens the children's eyes to the visual world that surrounds them. Some would argue that linking talking about the visual environment with corresponding experimental and investigative work in art is the key to creating visually literate children. This literacy benefits both art and language.

Even if the children are very experienced young artists it is still worth while thinking up a preparatory activity to revise work on a visual element, or simply to warm the children up to the new task.

## Talking about the experiments

Before the children begin to paint or draw the landscape, talk about the experimental work. Use these discussions to help suggest possible approaches to painting or drawing the landscape. Some advice about what to say to children before they begin work is detailed in the following paragraphs. If you were using the examples above you would be asking the children to focus on one of the visual elements. Adapt this way of working to any subject. Substitute your own topic for landscape and design a unit of work based upon the ideas described in this chapter.

Landscape drawing, colour and texture, Year 4

Using drawing boards outside

## ▏▏▏▏ Some advice for the children as they make their landscape drawing

As an example the text that follows assumes the children have been exploring shape and tone as starting points. The teacher has found a view point from which the children can draw a landscape. Drawing boards are an essential item of equipment if children are going to be comfortable when they are drawing (see page 123 in the materials appendix for advice on making drawing boards). Use masking tape to hold down the corners of the paper, especially on windy days.

"Look carefully at the landscape. What can you see that has shape? Where are the most noticeable shapes. Where are the darkest tones? Where are the deepest shadows? Where are there light tones? Can you see light? Remember to concentrate on showing the shapes and tones when you draw.

Find the view point you want to draw from. In which direction are you going to look? What is in the centre of the view you are looking at? What are you going to put in the centre of your drawing?

Find the centre of your paper. Start the drawing there. First, draw in an outline shape and then add in a few others around it.

Think about the size of your drawing and the size of your paper. How much of this view do you want to fit into your drawing? How big should your first shapes be?

Draw lightly to start with, when you think the size and position of your first few shapes is working well you can press harder to make stronger lines.

Work slowly towards the edges of the paper adding more shapes as you go.

After a while go back to the centre and start adding in extra details.

Start looking for the very dark tones, the deepest shadows and begin adding those into the drawing.

Can you draw in some of the medium tones, just like the ones you made when you were experimenting?"

Try giving the children drawing media to work with that they cannot rub out such as thin fibre tipped pens, black wax crayons, black marker pens and biros. Of course charcoal and chalk on off-white or buff paper would be suitable for drawings with a lot of tonal contrast.

Older children may complain about not being able to rub out their mistakes, but after a while this strategy can create much more confident and fluent drawings. If you want the children to use pencils you could ban the use of rubbers. Children who are drawing confidently will use rubbers with discretion so a ban could be a temporary measure. The danger of allowing unlimited use of rubbers right from the start is that some children are so worried about how their drawings are going to look that they never really do any drawing at all: their paper is just a mass of rubbings out. Making alterations, subtle rearragements and adjustments is a vital part of drawing, however, it is much more important first to build children's confidence to draw, to have a go. See page 83 for more advice about helping children with their fear of 'making mistakes'.

If you are using charcoal and chalk on mid-toned paper ask the children be careful about resting hands and arms on their drawings to avoid unwanted smudging. Remind them how useful chalk is for showing light.

If you are not using charcoal and chalk it is useful to point out that the children can leave the paper white if they need to show very light or very bright areas.

Children who bring you their drawings to comment on can be encouraged to look for more shapes or add in more tones. But there is a point at which children are just overwhelmed by too much looking. Many drawings work well without too much detail.

"Are you sure you have completely finished? Are there other shapes or tones you can add? Have you included all the important parts of the landscape? Is there a part of your landscape drawing that you can improve? Step back and take a moment to look at your drawing before you decide what to do next or if you are finished."

Adapt this advice for any of the visual elements that you may have used as starting points.

**Materials and Resources:**
Drawing boards and masking tape
A2 size paper
Appropriate drawing media, see advice above
Hair spray to fix charcoal and chalk

## ◗◗ Preparing to make a landscape painting, making a photomontage

Children could be working outside or working from drawings in their sketchbooks. They could work from larger drawings or photographs. Paintings made by simply copying a photograph can be very dull and lifeless. Discuss with the children experience of being in a landscape compared with that of looking at a photograph.

Landscape drawing, shape tone and texture, Year 6

Landscape painting, Year 5

"Here is a photograph of the landscape we are going to be painting. What are the main differences between the photograph and the real place? What can the photograph not show about what it is like to be in the landscape itself?"

It is important that the children have actually experienced the landscape they are painting. However, many artists use photographs as part of their investigation of a subject. Make a

photomontage of the landscape. You can do this by taking a series of photos from one spot, moving the camera each time so that the photos overlap at the edges. When the prints are processed the children can glue them on to a piece of card overlapping the edges to make a large landscape montage. This is helpful in providing useful visual information to aid work in the classroom or studio. It can never be a substitute for the experience of the landscape itself.

Give the children paper to use for testing out colours. Remind them about using the mixing palette, washing and wiping the brush to keep the colours looking clean. (See pages 39-41 of 'Teaching Art at Key Stage 1' for the kind of detailed information about this technique that can be given to younger or inexperienced children.)

Here is a reminder:

"Never put a dirty brush into the colour palette. You must always keep the colours you start with clean.

Always wash and wipe the brush.

Mix your colours on the mixing palette before painting on the paper.

Painting made in the landscape, Year 5

Remember to use different sizes of brush depending on whether you are painting large areas of colour or small details.

Only change the water when it is really dirty, when it looks like cold tea! You only need to wash your mixing palette if there is really no room for a brand new colour. Don't forget that you can mix wonderful new colours by changing colours you have already made. Try adding fresh colour on top of some of the old colours in your mixing palette."

The quality of the painting will be in direct relation to the quality of the preparatory experimental work, (see pages 47-50 for more ideas). It is assumed that the advice that follows will be given to children who have been exploring colour and shape in the landscape.

Materials and Resources:
All the equipment needed for colour mixing using paint, see text on this page (see also pages 123-124)

## ◗◗ Some advice for children as they make their landscape painting

"We have talked about the colour in the landscape, particularly differences between all the different greens, try to show that there are lots of different greens in your painting.

If you need to, use the scrap of paper to test out your colours first.

You have a thick and a thin brush, use the thick brush for large areas of colour and the thin brush for detail.

To start the painting, mix a very pale colour in the mixing palette and use the thin brush to paint in some outlines of the largest shapes. Only paint a few of these, there is no need to put in lots of detail. This is like drawing although you are using a paintbrush rather than a pencil. The idea is that you can plan what is going into the painting before you start. This means you need to think a little bit about where all the parts of the landscape are going to go on the paper. This is called 'composition'.

The great thing about painting is that it easy to make changes if you make a mistake or if you don't like a colour. Just mix some thicker paint and paint over the bits you don't like. You may need to wait a little if the paint on the painting is still very wet.

Many artists paint large patches of colour first and then gradually add more colour on top. They put detail in at the end. Other artists try to paint all parts of the painting quickly, in one go, they do not paint a background first. Every artist has a personal way of

doing things. There are many different techniques and styles of painting. Try and find a way to paint that suits you."

## ◗ Extending the children's painting experience

For more experienced children there are many different exercises that you could use to extend their experience of painting.

The children could experiment mixing and using thick and thin paint. They could experiment making different kinds of mark with the brush. These exercises could be linked to work on texture and work on line or mark.

Extend the children's awareness of colour with experimental and investigative work using complementary colours, warm and cold colours, bright and dull colours or concentrate on different colour families such as blues or the tertiary colours, the browns. Look back at page 49.

Importantly, much of the children's experience of drawing can be translated into painting; work on shape, space and line can also be important starting points for making landscape paintings.

Some teachers advocate using different kinds of paint such as water colours, poster paints, acrylic paints and even oil paints. Most of the basic exercises and starting points are just as valid what ever the media, and comparisons between how the different media behave can be illuminating. Some of these paints may be of high quality but they can be very expensive.

Children could experiment using different papers or cards for their paintings.

A mini landscape

Mini landscape with snail shells, Year 5

**Materials and Resources:**
All the equipment needed for painting, (see pages 55-56)
Different kinds of paints
Different kinds of brushes
Material to add to the paint to make it thicker, PVA for example
Material to give texture to the paint, sand for example
Different kinds of paper and card

## Other ideas for work linked to landscape

The photographs show children working on pastel drawings of indoor landscapes. They can create their own mini-landscapes with turf, stones, and pieces of plant material. The class were learning about snails so the empty snail shells were an obvious addition. The drawings were prompted by a discussion about what the landscape is like from a snail's point of view.

Stories that are read or made up by children can prompt work on imaginary or fantasy landscapes. There are many paintings by adult artists that will also inspire children to think up unusual ideas. All the preliminary experiments and investigations are just as valid for imaginary landscapes as those based on the real world. Ask the children to work on a range of different ideas in their sketchbooks before deciding on an approach for the painting itself.

Landscape colour can be used as a stimulus for weaving or fabric design. Very tactile woven objects can be made by using materials from the landscape itself, for example, creepers, grass, twigs, reeds, wool etc. Children could select the colours of different wools, threads or ribbons to give their weaving a similar feel to the landscape they observed. In this case considering landscape colour is very much part of a design process. For example, patterns for fabrics could be generated from research into landscape shape and colour.

Children could make relief prints inspired by landscape (see page 110) or adapt drawings for prints made with polystyrene tiles. Different media and techniques could be used to create different effects on the sugar paper which is then used for collage work (see page 46).

## Talking about landscape paintings or drawings by adult artists

Many of the preceding ideas can be used to help structure a discussion of the painting or drawing technique used by an adult artist. To summarise here are some of points that you could ask the children to comment on:

Differences between colours from the same family such as blues, browns or greens.

Warm and cool colours; bright and dull colours; light and dark colours.

The thickness or thinness of the paint.

The marks and lines the artist has used.

## **Practical exercises that start by talking about a painting**

Launch practical work on the visual elements by talking about a painting first. The children could go on to collect some of the colours and shapes they can see in the painting that has been discussed. They could show the different lines the artist has used or find a way to record the different tonal values of the painting. They could make their own drawing on a strip of paper of the all that they can see in the distance as they look into a landscape painting. Mark making experiments could be linked to discussions about textures and the kinds of marks the artist made with the brush.

### **Talking about landscape paintings focusing on content rather than technique**

The approach described above concentrates on some of the formal aspects of a painting or drawing, in other words how the painting works visually. Knowing about how artists made paintings look the way they do, by using tone, shape, colour and so on, helps the children understand how they can manipulate the same qualities in their own work. This way of understanding paintings and drawings will help children develop visual literacy, they will then become more comfortable using this visual language of art, craft and design.

However, it is difficult to separate how paintings and drawings look from their content and meaning. For example, landscape paintings can give children ideas about history (how the landscape might have changed); geography (rivers and mountains for example); biology (a wealth of flora and fauna). Landscape paintings may be imaginary and inspire links to story telling and fantasy. In other words it is important to discuss what the paintings show and the feelings generated by the work, it is important to discuss what the art expresses. All paintings, even abstract ones, show us ideas. With children in the classroom, teachers can help to illuminate some of the ideas visible in a painting by asking questions.

"What can you see when you look at the painting? Make a list of everything that comes to mind. Don't forget to mention the most obvious things as well.

What would it be like if you were standing in the painting? How would you feel?

What is going on around you?

What is the weather like?

Using a view finder to isolate a part of a painting

The textures on the surface of the painting; and textures of objects represented in paintings.

The shapes.

The space of the painting including points about foreground, middleground and background.

Light and dark parts of the painting; the light in the painting. Where is the light coming from?

Patterns in the painting.

**Materials and Resources:**
A selection of landscape paintings in reproduction, favourites include: Constable, Turner, Impressionists' landscapes, Van Gogh. Seek out some contemporary landscape paintings, paintings by women artists and landscapes from different cultures.
Visit an art gallery

### **Linking these discussions with the children's practical work**

Link any discussion of a painting with the children's own art work. Many projects could start by talking about a painting or drawing. Some teachers prefer to leave the discussion to the end of a related activity or even to the end of the whole project so that the solutions appropriate to adult artists do not influence the children too much.

If you could take a walk through the painting what would you pass? What would you see?
What mood does the painting make you think of?

Does the painting remind you of anywhere or anything?

What do you like about the painting?

What do you dislike?

Would you take the painting home and hang it up so you could see it every day? Think of a reason for your answer?

Can you summarise what you think about the painting?

## Other strategies for working with paintings and drawings

A rich language exercise can be planned by making comparisons between two or more landscapes.

Try looking at approaches to landscape in the work of artists from other cultures. For example, aboriginal Australians use pattern in work that is linked to their environment. In the last 30 years many British artists such as Richard Long and Andy Goldsworthy have been creating new forms of landscape inspired art, much of which relies heavily on pattern making. In this example the visual element of pattern links the work of artists from different cultures together. Try using the other visual elements to make appropriate visual links between different examples of art, craft and design.

Finally, here is a familiar idea for a lesson that might be used to help children investigate a painting:

A print of a painting was mounted on card.

A grid of squares or rectangles is then drawn over the print and cut out. The number of squares or rectangles depends on the number of children or groups taking part in the exercise.

Each child has one cut out piece of the painting and is asked to try to mix the colours visible in their section of the painting. In other words they have to copy their section on a new square or rectangle.

When all the pieces of the painting have been copied by the group or class it is reassembled and compared with the original. The project works well if the children do not know in advance what the completed painting looks like. Different children will have approached the task in different ways. Children will clearly see that each individual has a style of painting of their own.

Comparing landscape paintings

Landscape work inspired by Magritte, Year 6 (see page 101)

Sketchbook drawings looking for shapes in the head, Year 5

## Starting points

Look at the chapter on landscape drawing and painting beginning page 47. Much of the general advice about drawing and painting landscape is equally relevant to drawing and painting portraits. In particular look carefully at 'Some advice for the children as they make their landscape drawing' on page 53. What follows is an example of sessions that teachers choose or adapt to a unit of work on portraits. The first session is designed to help children to focus on the shapes they can see in a head. Begin this work by reminding the children about the concept of shape (see page 79).

## ❙❙ Collecting shapes from a head

Ask them to use their sketchbooks and collect some of the individual features (eyes, mouth, nose etc.) that make up the head.

"Look carefully at the shape of the nose, look at the nose from the side and from the front. Draw the nose in your sketchbook. Concentrate on the outline shape. Collect some other examples of the nose shapes. Look at eyes, mouths, ears, hair styles in the same way. Make sure you have several examples of each. Remember not to draw the whole portrait, just collect the shapes of the various features."

Portrait showing understanding of shape and tone, Year 5

## Starting with tone

Ask the children to make some tonal experiments. (See pages 24 and 50, also the chapter on tone in 'Teaching Art at Key Stage 1' pages 64-69.) If you are going to use pencils for the portrait drawing give the children a selection of different grades of drawing pencil, say 4B, 2B, HB and H. Ask them to experiment in their sketchbooks creating a series of tonal patches. Ask the children to comment on the relative qualities of the different pencils:

"Which of the media you used made the darkest tones? Which one made the faintest marks? Which pencil shows up the clearest?"

Materials and Resources:
Sketchbooks
Graded drawing pencils
Other drawing media

## Collecting tones from a head

"Look carefully at your partner's head. Where can you see the darkest tones? Are there any parts of the head that are black? Where can you see shadows? Where are the deepest shadows? Are there any areas of skin that are darker than others? Is the hair all exactly the same tone?

Use your sketchbooks and collect some of the shadows and dark parts of the head. For example just draw the shadows around the nose or under the mouth or around the ears. See if you can draw a nose or an eye or a mouth by using patches of different tones.

Practice drawing a small patch of skin or hair. Use the pencil to show how there are a number of different tones even in quite a small area of skin or hair. Just as before, don't draw the whole head. You are practising drawing tones."

The children's drawings may not look like anything very much, but they are focusing on tone and practising using appropriate drawing media.

Materials and Resources:
Sketchbooks
Graded drawing pencils
Other drawing media

## Starting with texture

Mirror the approach used above, but this time focus on the textural qualities of a head. For example, ask the children to use the drawing pencils to try and show the difference between skin and hair. Encourage the children to experiment with different ways of using the pencil until they have found a method that works well.

You could also look at clothing in this way. For example, ask the children to explore ways of recording the differences in texture between wool and polyester cotton.

Materials and Resources:
Sketchbooks
Graded drawing pencils
Other drawing media

Portrait showing an understanding of tone and texture, Year 5

## Starting with Colour

"Look at the back of your hand. What colours can you see? Use pastels or paint to try and mix some skin colours. Make a collection of colours in your sketchbook. Is there another way you could collect skin colours? Try cutting out different examples of skin colours from colour magazines. Glue fragments of skin colour into your sketchbooks."

Materials and Resources:
Sketchbooks
Soft pastels
Coloured pencils
Hair spray
All the equipment needed for mixing colours (see pages 55-56)

## Matching skin and hair colours

The children could go on to match some of the colours collected from magazines by mixing with pastels or paint.

Ask the each child to cut a large colour photograph of a head and shoulders in half, length ways. Use a photograph from a colour magazine.

Looking at portraits

Glue one half onto paper. Ask the children to complete the missing half in paint or pastels. How close can they come to matching the colours from the photograph?

Materials and Resources:
A3 or A2 paper
Drawing boards
Scissors
PVA
All the equipment needed for mixing colours (see pages 55-56)

### ◗◗Drawing the head and shoulders

Ask each child to find a partner. Each pair should have one drawing board and one set of drawing media between them. The children will take it in turns to be a model and an artist.

"Look carefully at the head of the model. What shape would you start with? Choose a shape from the middle of the head, the nose is a good place to start. Draw the shape of the nose just above the middle of your paper.

Look for some more shapes. How about the shapes that make up the eyes? Draw those in next. Keep looking and drawing until you have drawn the most important shapes from the head.

Look at the shapes of the clothing that the model is wearing. Look at the collar and the neck. Are there any patterns in the clothes you can see?

Look carefully at the shape of the chin, hair and eyebrows. Look carefully at the shape of the whole head. It is not an exact circle or oval, try and draw the shape that you can see.

Now look for shadows. Start by drawing in the very darkest tones. Then add in more shadows and tones from each part of the head."

This method is concentrating on shape and tone. You could use colour and texture as a focus or tone and colour, or shape and texture. Try asking older and more advanced children to work thinking about three or four basic elements, say, shape, tone, colour and texture.

Materials and Resources:
Drawing board
Masking tape
A3 or A2 paper
Graded drawing pencils
Other drawing media

### ◗◗◗Some advice for children drawing the portrait

"You will need to think big, Try to imagine the size of the head and shoulders on the paper. How big should your nose be? Start slowly and draw the first nose shape lightly. You can always make it bigger if it is too small to start with.

Look at the position of the eyes. If your partner is looking straight at you the eyes will be half way between the top of the head and the chin. Look for the position of the mouth. Look at where the hair line goes. Where are the tops and bottoms of the ears?

Even very experienced artists find drawing portraits difficult. You are bound to make mistakes. Sometimes your portrait might look strange. Don't worry, the more you practice the easier it will be to make a better drawing next time.

If you want your portrait to look a little like the model pick something that really stands out about who it is you are drawing. Is the hair style distinctive? Are the clothes noticeable? Is your partner wearing jewellery or anything in their hair? Concentrate hard on making your drawing look distinctive."

Challenge older and more advanced children by asking them to observe two or three children looking in different directions. One child could look straight ahead, another to the side and a third could be looking up or down. They will have to think carefully about the features and where they are in relation to each other. For example, if the head is tilted back the eyes may appear near the top of the outlined head in the drawings.

## Looking at portraits

Pick a selection of portraits by adult artists to show the children - postcards are useful for group work. But you may need larger prints if you wish to talk about the portraits with the whole class. Of course there is no substitute for visiting an art gallery to look at original portraits.

"What can you see when you look at each of the portraits? What are the people wearing? What is in the background and foreground of each portrait?

Talk about the different colours in each one."

The children could attempt to mix a selection of colours from each of the portraits.

"What sort of person is shown in the portrait? What character do you think they have? How are they feeling? How has the artist given the person in the portrait a character? How would you describe their expression?"

The children could collect some examples of different facial expressions in their sketchbooks.

"Which is the best painting we have talked about? Which would you choose to put up on a wall at home? What are the reasons for your choice? Do you think a friend would chose a different painting?"

Materials and Resources:
Sketchbooks
Drawing media
A selection of portraits by adult artists: Rembrandt, Van Gogh and artists from Renaissance Italy are popular examples from our culture. Search out some portraits by contemporary artists. Extend the project by looking at portraits and heads drawn by artists from different cultures.

## Drawing a portrait inspired by the style of an artist

Ask the children to make a portrait of their partner in the style of one of the portraits they have been talking about. It is important to spend some time discussing the characteristics of the artist's work. The nineteenth century artist Renoir used a technique and colour very different to Francis Bacon's portraits from the last part of this century. As an example of how one artist can use different approaches through a life time, Picasso's early cubist portraits are very different from ones made later in his life. Artists from different cultures approach portraiture in very different ways from western Europeans. It is helpful to compare different approaches so that children can make an informed choice about the 'style' they would like to adopt for their own work.

Portrait in the style of Welsh artist John Petts

A painted portrait, Year 6

They do not need to mimic everything about the style of a chosen artist. Ask the children to pick one or two characteristics of their favourite portrait to use in their own drawing. They could choose the background or the style of clothing. Perhaps they could try to use the colour scheme or even similar lines and marks to the ones the artist used. Oil pastels are a good medium to use for this activity. They have a richness of colour and allow for different methods of application.

## ▶ Painting a portrait

The class can go on to paint a portrait. Ask the children to follow some of the steps outlined in this chapter but using paint rather than drawing media. A key to working in paint is to think of it as a natural extension to drawing. Make sure that the children learn to draw in paint with a brush, rather than drawing in pencil first and then filling colours with paint. Ask them to start their portrait by mixing a very pale colour in the mixing palette. They can draw some of the important shapes in their portrait with a thin brush, using this pale colour. Encourage the children to paint over mistakes. Once children are happy to paint one colour over another their painting will quickly become more fluent. Much of the advice appropriate to painting landscapes could be repeated here, look back at page 56.

Portrait, Year 5

**Materials and Resources:**
All the equipment needed for painting (see pages 55-56)

## Building confidence

This project works best if the children are confident about drawing shape. (See page 79 for detailed advice about how to help children revise this vital concept.)

Confidence is always an issue when drawing figures, it is natural for both children and teachers to want the drawings to look real, like real people. Naturally, children in primary school are inexperienced artists and so as yet they have not the skills or the experience to draw with a conventional realism. It is important that they understand that they are only learning about drawing and just as with all new and difficult tasks, they need practice. Skill and facility are artistic qualities that develop slowly backed up by a great deal of practice. Education in music or sport encourages a great deal of practice that is sometimes very repetitious, children often find it

boring even if adults emphasise its necessity. Art education specialists look upon repetition and technical practice for its own sake with suspicion. No matter what our views are about the relative merits of purely technical exercises there is no doubt that the limited time available for art in school is best used to give children a broad base of experience. This means that children will not often have the opportunity to practice drawing figures. Teachers should help them to understand that they will find it very hard to draw figures accurately or realistically. But it is good to try and paying attention to the visual elements will help children find an angle, a focus that will improve their drawings. As the children grow older and have more opportunities to practice drawing, they will find that just as in all their work, they will improve and grow in confidence.

The emphasis on 'shape' in the landscape, portrait and figure work is deliberate. This simple to

What shapes can you make with your body?

## Looking for the outline shapes of figures

You might begin this project by drawing around body shapes with chalk on in the playground. This will help to reinforce the concept of shape in relation to the outlines of figures. The children will see the huge variety of shapes a figure can make - time spent looking and discussing will be well rewarded. Use volunteers to demonstrate the many different kinds of shapes the body can make.

"She has made her body into a shape that reminds me of a bridge. Can anyone else think of a different shape that they could make with their bodies? Come out and show us.

This body shape looks very sad. Someone who looked like this might be very unhappy. Can you think of any other emotions that we can show with our bodies? Try happy, excited, nervous. Now for ideas of your own."

The children can act out these shapes in groups or work out a number of ideas on their own. This can become part of a wider project. (See page 115 in the section that describes an issue led project with the theme of war and fear.)

Materials and Resources:
Chalk to draw around children lying in the playground
A camera to photograph some of their body shapes

## Drawing the body shapes

Ask for volunteers to pose in one of the shapes the children discovered. They can now draw the outline of the figure in their sketchbooks. Ask them not to put too much detail in, there is no need to draw eyes, noses, mouths and so on. It is the outline that is important. Remind them not to worry about mistakes. It is important that all the class or group can see the model. Improvise a table as a stage or use a large open space for this work such as the hall or the playground. There can be a number of different drawings on each side of their paper.

Materials and Resources:
Sketchbooks and drawing media

## Drawing four different views of the same figure

Choose one of the poses and place the model in the middle of the room. All the children should be sitting facing the model. A circle works well. Give each child a strip of paper which can be folded into quarters length ways. The model will have to pose four times, each time she should face in a different direction (North, South, East and West).

What shapes can you make with your body?

understand concept can be used as an underlying foundation to help children draw many of the familiar subjects they will come across in school. Children will soon recognise that concentrating on shape can underpin their drawing. It will become natural and normal for children to look for shapes when they draw. The other visual elements can inter-link with and develop out of a confidence gained from children's increasingly articulate drawing of shape.

## Warming up with shapes

Use one of the warm up exercises to help the children refocus on shape. Even if the children are experienced artists it is still helpful to find a way to revise this concept. (Look at pages 79-80 for more ideas.)

Figure drawing that expresses an emotion, Year 5

"Draw the outline shape of the model on the first quarter of your paper. When everyone has finished, we will change the view point you have of the figure by asking the model to make the same pose but facing a different way. You only need draw what you can see. Do not draw anything you cannot see. If you have a back view or a side view draw that. You will have four different drawings of the same pose."

This can be hard work for the model! This exercise is also relevant to developing an understanding of space in drawing in relation to the view point of the artist.

**Materials and Resources:**
Sketchbooks and drawing media
Strips of paper folded into four
Drawing boards and masking tape

## Talking about figure drawings

Artists from many different eras and cultures have drawn the human figure. It is not difficult to find different examples to show the children. The Renaissance artists from Italy produced many figure drawings. The best examples to use are from sketchbooks. Look for the figure drawings of Leonardo, Michelangelo and Raphael. You could research figure drawings by contemporary British artists. For example, the work of Paula Rego would be useful here. Some of these drawings were often made very quickly. The children can see that even famous artists make 'mistakes'.

Photocopy some of the drawings and display them with the children's work.

The way we use the words 'shape' and 'form' is confused in the English language. Adults as well as children find it difficult to work out what is meant by the word 'form'. The form of a figure is the shape it takes in three dimensions. However, as we have seen figures drawn on paper have a two dimensional shape. However it is possible for two dimensional drawings to show form. To help clarify this for children at Key Stage 1 and 2 reserve the word 'form' for talking about objects in three dimensions and only use the word 'shape' when you mean a shape in two dimensions.

**Materials and Resources:**
Figure drawings by a variety of artists

## Revising tone

Remind the children about tone - light and dark. Try a simple warm up exercise (see pages 24, 50 and 63). If children are using charcoal and chalk, the mixing needed in this exercise can be subtle, so even if they are very experienced with this media it well worth setting some time aside for practising delicate mixes of black and white.

**Materials and Resources:**
Charcoal and chalk
Buff, grey or off white sugar paper
Hair spray to fix the experiments

Figure drawing that expresses an emotion, Year 5

Using stocking net to simplify the shape and form

## Using stocking net to simplify the shape and form

The following sequence of activities builds on what has gone before. You will need stocking net which you can buy by the yard from ironmongers. You can use this exercise to introduce older children to the relationship between shape and form.

Ask for a volunteer to try on the stocking net, it is an elasticated tube that will slip over the head and can be dragged down to the feet. It is better if the whole body is hidden by the net. Tie a knot in the top, tuck the bottom end under the child's feet.

"What can you see? How would you describe the body sculpture? What has happened to the body? What can't you see? What does the body remind you of?"

Ask the model to try different poses. For example, ask the child inside the tube to push out their hands, or bend in different ways. Ask the other children for more ideas about what the model can do. You will find some interesting effects using different props like furniture or apparatus from the hall. The children can take it in turns to pose. Try posing two or three children together!

The activity could have a definite focus, for example you could talk about an emotion like sorrow. How can the figure, wrapped in the elastic net appear sorrowful? You could refer to the figures as body sculptures.

Materials and Resources:
Stocking net and a variety of props
Use a camera to record the various poses

## Drawing the body sculptures

Choose a pose to draw. Organise the children to draw as above. This time, before they draw, remind them about tone. Ask them to look at the figure and decide where the lightest tones are and where the darkest tones are. Remind them about shape. Choose a paper that is neutral in colour and tone, perhaps light grey or buff sugar paper.

"Use charcoal and chalk to draw the body sculpture. Use the chalk to draw the shape very lightly at first, if you make a mistake you can easily redraw a new shape over the first one. Use the chalk again to show the light tones. Then use the charcoal to show dark tones, look for shadows. You will need to be careful about how you use the charcoal with the chalk, work slowly and think carefully about the greys you need to make."

The children can go on to draw groups of body sculptures. Or perhaps they could work on one large drawing rather than a series of small ones.

**Materials and Resources:**
Stocking net and a variety of props
Charcoal and chalk
Grey, buff or off white sugar paper
Drawing boards and masking tape
Hair spray to fix the drawings

## Talking about the sculptures and drawings of Henry Moore

Many teachers would introduce this at the start of the project, and this can also work well. Here, the idea is that children are not influenced by Moore's drawings in advance but come to understand something of his work after their own attempts. Moore was first and foremost a sculptor and his drawings are often very tonal, he used contrasts between light and dark to represent three dimensional form in two dimensions. The idea here is that shadows and highlights help to show the form of figures. For example, the figures look rounded rather than flat. This can be complicated to explain to children but this project is designed

Stocking net body sculpture

partly to make the point in a practical way. Older and more experienced children will be fascinated. After looking at and talking about the drawings show the children examples of Moore's sculptures. Talk about the similarities between their drawings of the body sculptures and Moore's work.

**Materials and Resources:**
A book about Henry Moore that includes examples of both his drawings and his sculptures

Drawing the body sculptures, Year 6

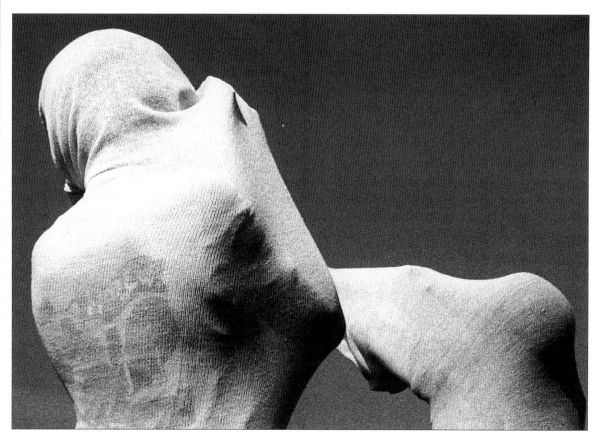

Using stocking net to simplify shape and form

# Figures and heads in clay

## ❚❚ Learning about clay

Even Year 6 children will need to experience some of the simple properties and possibilities of clay if they are new to the media. Here is an example of how a teacher might explain some important points about using clay to the class. (The same basic technique for using clay was described in 'Teaching Art at Key Stage 1', pages 50-52.)

"We have laid builder's polythene over the tables to keep them clean and make tidying up easier. We have taped the polythene to the table with masking tape to stop it slipping. On the polythene are wooden boards to work on.

You will also need a paper towel. Sometimes the clay sticks to the boards. If you think this is going to be a problem put your work on one of the paper towels. You can also slide and turn the work around by moving the paper towel. This means that you don't have to keep picking up your sculptures, which is a

Imaginary clay head

problem if the clay is soft and the sculptures are delicate. You can easily damage what you have just made.

There are some tools you can use to cut or change the clay in different ways.

Each of you has a lump of clay to work with. The clay is wrapped in a small polythene food bag ready for you to use. Why do you think we need to keep clay wrapped up like that?

There is also a sponge on the table. The sponge is damp, but it is not wringing wet. As you use the clay it will begin to dry out. If the clay is too dry it will begin to crack and crumble and become difficult to use. You can often tell if this is likely to happen by looking at your hands, if the clay on your hands is turning lighter and feeling dry and dusty it is probable that the clay you are using is also too dry. What do you think would happen if we just added water to the clay? The danger is that the clay becomes so wet and sticky that not only is it difficult to make anything good but everything, including you, gets in a terrible mess. You should never just add water to the clay. If your hands feel dry just press them onto the damp sponge and keep on working. That is just enough dampness to keep the clay in the right condition so that it is easy to use.

On the table is some slip together with an old paint brush. The slip is a mixture of clay and water, it has the consistency of double cream. You need to use the slip like a glue. If you ever need to join two pieces of

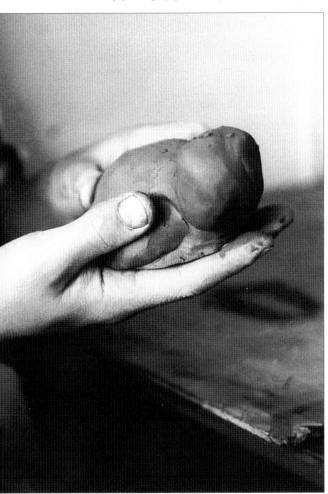

Working with clay

clay together use the paintbrush and the slip. Use the slip like glue to make sure you sculptures do not fall apart when they dry. You will also need to press the pieces of clay firmly together.

Look out for little bits of clay that break off. These can fall on the floor or clutter up your working space. Try to collect all the little bits of clay every now and then while you are working. Artists know how important it is to keep their work space organised and tidy."

## A simple science experiment to observe changes in clay

Design a simple experiment that will help children to understand what happens to clay as it dries out over a period of time. Try leaving clay out in the classroom and for comparison wrap clay in a sealed polythene bag. Try leaving clay outside or in a cool damp place. Leave clay in different containers, some with lids, some without. Ask children to look out for changes in colour, how the clay feels and any changes to the containers themselves. A container with a lid on may show condensation as water evaporates out of the clay.

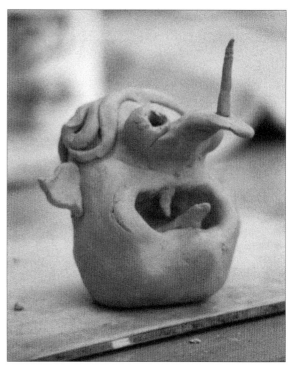

Small clay head, Year 5

## Starting with simple forms

If the children are using clay for the first time, or it has been quite a while since it was last used, ask them to experiment by making simple three dimensional forms such as cuboids, cylinders, spheres, pyramids etc. When they have a collection of simple forms they can use the slip to join them together to make a sculpture. This is a three dimensional version of the activity where simple two dimensional shapes are used to make pictures. The children will quickly discover that they can assemble the basic three dimensional forms into clowns, trains, cars, rockets, robots, aliens and so forth.

Materials and Resources:
All the equipment needed for using clay ( see page 73)

## Making small figures in clay or plasticine

The drawing activities on pages 68-71 are the starting points for this project.

plasticine is also a good media to use for making small figures. With plasticine the work can be developed into an animation project.

There are two ways the children can explore making figures in clay. It is worth explaining both methods because most children will use a combination of the two.

"Here is a ball of clay, it is quite small so your figures will only be about 10cm long. Try to make the form

Making a small figure in clay

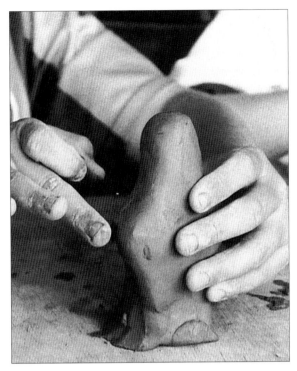

Small clay figure, Year 5

of a body. Then see if you can squeeze out the arms, legs and a head. Go slowly, try not to make the legs and arms so thin that they fall off. If your figure is not coming out well just squash the clay into a ball and try again. Don't forget to use the sponge to moisten your hands if the clay gets too dry.

Which of the simple forms do arms and legs remind you of? Yes, long cylinders. Now try modelling the head and body out of one lump of clay and then use more clay to make the arms and legs separately, use the slip to join them to the body."

The children will come across many problems. The legs and arms will be too thin and fall off. They will try to stand their figures up and the legs will just not be strong enough. Warn them in advance about the problems and discuss possible solutions. Or suggest that they have two separate attempts at the activity, the first to find out about the problems, the second to see if they can work out solutions. If you have given the children the opportunity to try out both methods of making a small figure, it is likely that they will end up using a combination of the two to make their own mini-figure sculptures.

"Now you are getting the hang of making small figures, think about the pose you would like your figure to have. What is your figure doing? What is your figure feeling? Could you work together and use all the figures to make one group? Is there anything else that you could make to go with the figure? Sometimes combining two or more figures or making some props will help support the sculptures."

Warn the children that however careful they have been, the clay figures may crack as they dry.

Materials and Resources:
All the equipment needed for using clay (see page 73)

## ❚❚ Using the stocking net drawings and the sculptures of Henry Moore as a prompt for figure sculptures

Look back to page 70. Start with that work and repeat the preceding figure project only this time ask the children to simplify the form of the figures. They will make their own small figure sculptures that may be influenced by Henry Moore's sculptures.

Go on to ask the children if they can think of other ways that they could change the form of their figure sculptures. Show them the work of Giacometti, Barbara Hepworth and Anthony Gormley. Introduce them to examples of how other cultures have made figure sculptures, for example, show the children pictures of the figures from Easter Island.

Materials and Resources:
All the equipment needed for using clay (see page 73)
Illustrations of figure sculptures by artists such as Moore, Hepworth, Giacometti and Gormley
Examples of figure sculptures from other cultures
The children's own figure drawings

## ❚ Making Heads in Clay

The starting point for this project may be portrait drawing (see page 64). Or you could begin by showing the children sculptural heads. The children's clay heads could be imagined or based on observation. The project can easily be adapted to a specific theme. For example, the children could make their own sculptures of Mr and Mrs Twit (see page 24).

This is one of those rare projects where it is necessary to be able to demonstrate the process in advance, but it is not difficult to do. This is how a teacher might describe the process to the children. Part of the introduction should focus on the fact that children will be working in the round. They will be able to consider the head from different angles and view points.

"We are going to make a head and shoulders in clay. What will be the differences between a head made out of clay and one drawn on paper? What will be good about making heads in clay instead of drawing?

As well as the clay and the usual equipment we are also going to need newspaper, masking tape and paper bags. This is a piece of cardboard that we can use as a base for the sculpture.

Put three sheets of newspaper together. Cut a long strip about 10cm wide.

Roll the strip into a tube. Use the masking tape to stop the tube unravelling.

At one end of the tube make about four short cuts. Bend the newspaper back to make tabs. Use the masking tape to tape these tabs flat onto the cardboard base so the tube stands up. This is the support for the neck.

Roll up a sheet of newspaper into a ball. Put it into the paper bag to stop it unravelling. Now tape the open end of the bag around the top of the tube. Use plenty of tape. This is the support for the head.

I have cut some thin sheets or clay from the clay bag using this cheese wire.

Mould the sheets of clay around the tube to make the neck. Now use more clay to make the shoulders. Do that now to give the neck support.
Use more thin sheets of clay to mould around the paper head. Smooth down the joins as you go. Take care to make sure the head is well joined to the neck.

Check to see if any of the newspaper or bag are showing. If this is happening, cover up the gaps with more clay. Are you happy with the general form of the shoulders, neck and head? Now is the time to make changes. You can be quite rough with the clay because at the moment there are no delicate features to spoil.

Now we can add the features. Think about where the eyes should go, not too near the top of the head! Use your thumbs to press in the eye sockets. Roll some clay to make the eye balls. Don't forget to use the slip.

Make a nose and use the slip to fix it to the head. Use a clay tool to press in a line for the mouth.

Add on lips, ears, eyebrows, nostrils.

Now look carefully at your clay head. Think about the chin, the forehead, the cheekbones. Turn the head around. Are you pleased with the form of the back of the head? Make any changes or additions you think are needed. Has the head got an expression, can you tell what sort of a character your head has? You may want to change some of the features to give more character or more expression to the sculpture.
Now you can add the hair. Use thin strips of clay and the slip. Perhaps you can give you head a hairstyle. Is the hair curly, straight, plaited, dreadlocked?"

As that is a lot of information all in one go it might be better to make the heads in stages, or at least

Making the paper neck and head

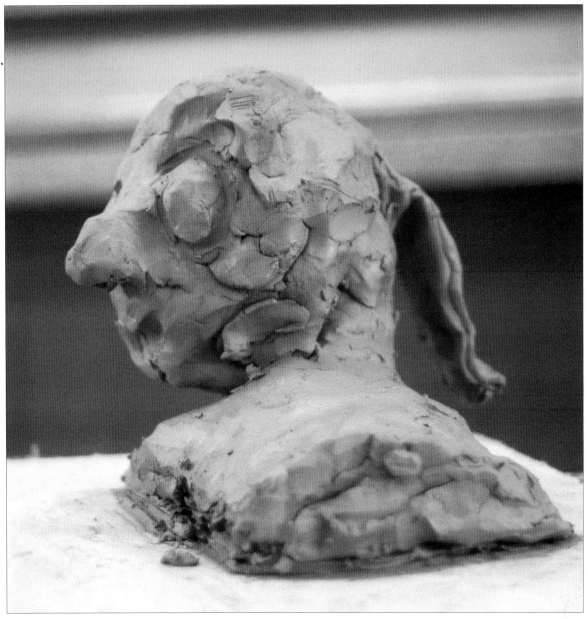

Clay head ,Year 5

to give the instructions in stages. If you need to spread this making activity over a number of days, spray the head with a plant mister at the end of each session and cover the head with a plastic bag, tucking the ends under the cardboard base. The clay will be fine as long as it is kept damp.

Another technique that can be used to make larger imaginary creatures or figures is based on the principle of coiling clay. The children do not use a paper support for their work, instead they build the basic structure by building up coils of clay. The illustration shows an imaginary figure or creature being made in this way. (See pages 54-56 of 'Teaching Art at Key Stage I' for information about introducing to young children the technique of coiling clay.)

**Materials and Resources:**
All the equipment needed for using clay (see page 73)
Newspaper
Masking tape
Scissors
Paper bags

Clay head ,Year 5

Making an imaginary creature by coiling the clay, Year 6

## ❘ Firing and glazing the heads

It is not possible here to give detailed information about firing and glazing. Seek advice from the art department in your local comprehensive, tertiary college or college of further education. Some potters will agree to fire work for a small charge. Firing and glazing clay creates new opportunities to help children understand how different processes affect and change materials that artists use to make art and design. This means that the characteristics of a chosen process will be very important when thinking about the way an end product may look.

If the heads are to be fired, gently remove the paper support from inside when the heads are dry. Most of it will pull out. Don't worry too much if some remains inside, it will burn away in the kiln.

Although this is quite a technical project and the activity is prescribed to some extent, the confidence that teachers and children will get from seeing the heads develop is worth the effort. It may be argued that it is better that the children work in this media in this way than to deny them opportunity for purely technical reasons. The technique may not be perfect, the end products may be flawed in the eyes of an expert but the value of the experience is undeniable.

A drawing of a bungalow, Year 2

## Revising the concept of shape using 'Teaching Art at Key Stage 1'

Children should be familiar with the visual elements from their work during Key Stage 1, however the concepts may need to be revised. If children at Key Stage 2 have never worked in this way before then it will be necessary to find a way of helping them to focus on shape. This basic investigative and explorative work underpins many of the projects in this book. Because this is so important, the following four short sections are reprinted from pages 14, 15 and 16 of 'Teaching Art at Key Stage 1'. Remember that the text in these sections was written with Reception and Year 1 children in mind. The drawing illustrated on this page is by a six year old child who worked through the four following sessions before making an observational drawing of the bungalow.

## ❙ Talking About Shapes

"Look around the room. Can you see any shapes? Let's make a list of the shapes you can see. Who can see a shape that is bigger than I am? Who can see a shape that is smaller than your hand?"

Children will immediately think of the shapes they have learnt in maths. The first step here is to link the shapes they know about through maths with the shapes of different things they can see in the room.

## ❙❙ Drawing around shapes and finding out about outlines

"Look. Here is a shape from the shape tray. I can draw a line around this shape. This is an outline. I can find the outline of all sorts of things. What shall I try next? A spoon? A key? Let's try a few more.

These outlines make shapes. Look at the shapes we have drawn. What can you recognise? We can recognise an object by its shape. Now you can draw around more things to make shapes of your own."

After you have made a few outlines with the children ask them to collect some more of their own. Provide a collection of interesting objects, or the children could hunt around the classroom and discover shapes for themselves. Afterwards they could try and guess the names of the objects that go with the outlines that other children collected.

Materials and Resources:
A large sheet of paper on an easel
A4 paper and clipboards or sketchbooks
Drawing media that make good clear outlines

## ❙❙ Finding shapes by looking

The children have been drawing around objects to make shapes. The next sequence of activities should help them collect different outlines by looking and drawing.

Shapes from a sketchbook, Year 1

"I want to collect the shape of the large window in the classroom. What are the problems? Can I put the window on my paper and draw around it? Why not?

Look! If I close one eye and point at the window I can trace around the outside of the frame to draw a shape in the air. Let's all practice.

Now here is a black wax crayon. I can look at the window and instead of tracing around the frame with my finger in the air I can draw the shape with the crayon on the paper. This time I am using my finger and I am drawing on the paper not in the air. I have to look carefully at the shape of the window.

Look at the shape I have drawn. Now you can collect the shapes of anything you want. Just look carefully and trace around the shape in the air with your finger and then draw the outline on the paper. Let's try and draw the shape of this teapot together.

Tell me some of the other things in the room you could find outline shapes for."

## ❙❙ Collecting shapes by looking and drawing

"Now you can hunt around the classroom and collect different outlines by looking and drawing. See how many you can collect. Don't draw too much detail inside your shape, it's the outline that's important."

The children could collect shapes of things much bigger than they are or they could collect shapes of things outside. The children should look carefully but at the same time not worry about making mistakes. The important thing is that they are looking at and drawing shapes. If they make attractive drawings that is a bonus. Soon they won't need to trace the shapes with their fingers they will just look and draw.

Materials and Resources:
A4 paper and clipboards or sketchbooks
A thin fibre tipped pen, black wax crayon or biro, these drawing media cannot be rubbed out and make a good clear dark line

## ❙❙ Collecting shapes inside shapes

This is also a revision exercise that can follow on from the above.

"Now I would like you to find some objects or images that have smaller shapes that are contained inside larger outline shapes. Who can think of some ideas? The computer key board is a good example.

Now try and collect a few examples in your sketchbooks. Draw in the larger outline shape first and then put in the smaller shapes you can see inside."

Collecting shapes inside

### )))Looking for shapes in buildings

You will need to take the children to look at a building or buildings. The school building is an obvious choice but there may be houses, shops, factories and places of worship that can be seen without even leaving the school playground.

"When you look at the building, where can you see shapes? What parts of the building have a shape? Are there examples of shapes that have smaller shapes inside them? Are any of the shapes repeated to make patterns?"

### )))Collecting building shapes by drawing

"In your sketchbooks draw some of the shapes you can see when you look at the building. Don't draw all the building. You may need to draw some shapes inside shapes too. Don't spend too long on any one drawing. It is important to collect a variety of different shapes."

It is possible to make this exercise quite structured. For example, if the children are looking at a variety of buildings they could collect window shapes, followed by door and doorway shapes, followed by roof shapes and so on. It is important that they don't try to draw the whole building at this stage, they are still investigating and still gaining experience of architectural shapes which will be invaluable as the project progresses. Ask the children also to look carefully for some of the smaller objects that are found on buildings. The shapes of alarms, grills, drainage pipes, aerials, satellite dishes, name plates, door furniture and much else can all be collected in the sketchbooks.

Materials and Resources:
Sketchbooks and drawing media

### )))Collecting patterns from buildings

As well as investigating different architectural shapes, the children could also explore the patterns they can see when looking at a building. They could collect examples of patterns in the same way as above. Ask them to draw just enough of the pattern to be able to recognise it clearly as a pattern, there is no need to draw it all. Younger children might need to do some simple revision about repeating patterns (see pages 26-29 from

Using sketchbooks to collect shapes from buildings

'Teaching Art at Key Stage 1'). Also look back at pages 31-33 in this book for other ideas about developing children's awareness of pattern.

Materials and Resources:
Sketchbooks and drawing media

### ⦚ Investigating colours, textures, tones, lines and marks

Each of these visual concepts could become the focus of further investigations of buildings.

The children could try to mix some of the different colours they can see in the building or they could collect some of the textures by making rubbings or plasticine prints (see page 73 from 'Teaching Art at Key Stage 1').

Ask them where they can see lines in the building. The children could practice drawing different lines and then try out different marks to show textures (see pages 70 and 71 from 'Teaching Art at Key Stage 1').

Talk with the children about all the darkest parts of the building and then discuss the lightest parts they can see. Ask them where they can see shadows? The children could now make some quick tonal drawings of small sections of the building in their sketchbooks. There are examples on pages 24, 50 and 63 of ways of helping children explore the concept of tone.

In all these examples of investigative work the emphasis is on exploring and experimenting rather than making good looking end products.

Materials and Resources:
Sketchbooks and drawing media appropriate to each investigation. Use soft pastels to collect colours, charcoal and chalk or soft drawing pencils to record tones. Wax crayons may be needed to make rubbings.

### ⦙ Making an observational drawing of a building

You have decided which building or buildings the children are going to draw. It is important that they are comfortable when they are working outside so they may need something to sit on. They will all need to be able to see the building clearly. If they want to make a larger drawing you will need to use the drawing boards. If there is any wind at all use masking tape to hold the corners of the paper. The children can easily prepare their own boards in this way. The masking tape can be peeled off carefully without tearing the drawing.

The children might use fibre tipped pens to draw with because then they will not be able to rub the ink out. Alternatives include black wax crayons, charcoal, even black biros. Drawing with materials like these is an effective strategy if children are nervous about drawing and inclined to use rubbers a lot. Some children spend so much time rubbing out their mistakes that they hardly do any drawing at all! The following paragraphs describe

Collecting shapes from buildings

Observational drawing, Year 4

some of the strategies that may help children feel more confident about their drawing.

Materials and Resources:
Drawing boards and making tape
A2 or A3 drawing paper
Appropriate drawing media, see above

## Talking about making mistakes

"Who plays a musical instrument? What was it like when you first started learning? Did you make lots of mistakes? What did the tune you were playing sound like? Who has been playing a musical instrument for while? What is it like when you try to play a new piece for the first time? Do you still make mistakes? What do you need to do to get better? Practice?

Drawing is just the same, even artists who have been drawing a long time make lots of mistakes, especially if it is a new way of drawing or if they are trying something they have not drawn before. Everybody will make mistakes. Don't worry about them too much.

If you think you have made a mistake at the start of your drawing it sometimes looks dreadful and you

will think, 'I have ruined my work already.' What you should do is forget about the mistake and keep going because by the end of the drawing it will not look nearly so obvious.

There will always be parts of the drawing that you think look good and parts that you are not so pleased with. Your drawing will not be perfect. Although some people are better at drawing than others everybody will improve if they practice. So, don't worry about your mistakes."

Such talk will not soothe the fear of drawing in every child but you will be trying to promote confidence and fluency. It is worth persevering with this approach and the fibre tipped pens because, after a while, the children will become used to this way of working and quickly settle down to draw. When they have gained the confidence to draw fluently you could give them pencils to draw with again. The children will also enjoy your enthusiasm for their drawing even if it is not to your taste as an adult. There is also a discussion on page 54 of issues concerned with helping children feel confident about drawing.

## Starting the drawing

"Find the middle of your paper. Look at the building, find a shape near the middle of the building. Try starting the drawing by putting that first shape in the middle of the paper. Next, look for the shapes that are nearby the first one and then add those to your drawing. Your drawing will grow bit by bit as you add in more of the shapes you can see. Don't forget that

Drawing patterns from the environment

most of the shapes will have other shapes inside them. Think carefully about where each new shape should go. Only draw the outline shape of the whole building after you have drawn most of the important window and door shapes."

## Another way to start the drawing

Using this strategy the children will need pencils and rubbers, but only to start with.

"Use the pencil very lightly. Draw the shape of the whole building onto your paper. Think carefully about

how big the building is going to look on the paper. Don't draw any detail with the pencil. The idea is that you are planning how the building is going to fit on the paper. You could add in one or two windows or a door, think about how big the windows and doors should be and where they are going inside the main shape of the building. Remember don't spend too long on the planning, there is no need to draw any detail with the pencil."

If the children are using large sheets of paper you may need to ask them to think big. There may be more than one building or other things that they would like to include in the drawing, they could draw the outline shapes of these in as well. When they are happy with how it all fits on the paper you should collect the pencils and rubbers and the children can start to draw with the fibre tipped pens. Just as in the first example, encourage them to draw the smaller shapes, working in the middle of the drawing first. Tell them that they will be able to rub out the pencil lines when they have finished. If you use this strategy it is important that the children do the minimum of the pencil planning. The idea is just to help them fit the drawing into the space of the paper.

## Working on the drawing

"Keep looking for all those shapes. Do you remember the patterns you found? You could add in some of the patterns too."

Advanced children may well have done recent work with textures, tones and lines and marks. If you think it is appropriate you could ask them to think about showing the dark parts of the building in their drawing, or they could add in any textures they can see, particularly the textures of the surface of the building itself. But for the younger or less advanced child it may be more than enough just to concentrate on shape.

## Finishing the drawing

Do the children want to put a background to their drawing? Have you talked with them about all that is in front of, above, behind or beside the building? This involves talking about the space that surrounds the building, space being another of the basic visual concepts (see page 51 for ideas about drawing space in terms of the forground and background).

If you feel a child could work for longer on their drawing, ask them to look for extra shapes or patterns, particularly within the architectural details. Or encourage them to add more shapes and patterns from the area around the building.

## Drawing urban landscapes

The strategy outlined in the previous sections can be used to help children draw an urban landscape which is full of different buildings. The emphasis in the discussion prior to drawing could be on how there are a large number of shapes within the view across the town.

The children could begin by using their sketchbooks to collect the shapes of all the different buildings they can see (look at page 81). When they start to draw the urban environment the most helpful method is to start in the middle of the paper with a shape and add others in turn to make a kind of patchwork of shapes as the drawing spreads across the paper.

When drawing landscapes of any kind starting the exercise with some experimental work on lines will also be very useful (see page 51).

## Developing the drawings into paintings

All the work in this chapter refers to drawing buildings, however, the same stategies could be used to develop paintings of buildings or urban landscapes. The sketchbook work, photographs or the finished drawings themselves might become source material that helps children approach a painting. (Look at pages 54-56 in the chapter on landscape painting and adapt that advice for this subject matter.)

## Talking about buildings

You can talk about real buildings or buildings in reproduction. The best strategy is to have two or more buildings to compare. For example a Victorian house compared with a modern home from an estate nearby; a Tudor fortified house compared with a Roman villa; a Jewish temple compared with a mosque and a church or chapel. You could look at public rather than private buildings; industrial buildings compared with shops, or perhaps you could talk about two or more well known buildings from the locality. The children could compare the buildings that they use and live in with buildings from different countries and cultures.

The following sequence of questions fall into roughly four groups. Although this is described in a way that is suitable for whole class discussion, why not ask groups of children to discuss similar questions written down for them in advance. They could go on to compose a more formal piece of writing about buildings.

"Tell me what can you see when you look at the front of this building?"

In each case ask the children this very simple question. Encourage them to mention all the obvious things as well as the more subtle points. The children will always find far more to talk about than one person will ever think of on their own. A useful strategy is to keep a list of what the children say they can see. It can provide a very useful prompt for describing the building in more detail later.

"Talk about the shapes, patterns, colours or textures can you see."

You could work through shape, pattern, colour and texture in turn. The children could simply talk about what they can see or they could link the discussion with a practical activity. They could collect shapes or patterns as on page 81. They could mix the colours they can see in the different buildings. They could collect some of the surface textures of the different building materials used by

Industrial landscape, Year 6

taking rubbings or plasticine prints, they could experiment with different drawing media to try and find marks that show the different textures (see pages 70-77 'Teaching Art at Key Stage 1').

"How does this building make you feel? What happens in this building?"

Urban landscape, Year 6

These questions are about establishing the character of each building. It is a way of discussing what values the architecture might communicate. Here are some more suggestions:

> "As you stand in front of this building what impression do you get? How does the building make you feel? Is this feeling different from the other building we looked at? How? What would you think if you used this building every day? What would it be like to live in a building like this? What about the windows and door ways, are they different to the ones you have at home? How are they different? Does the building remind you of anything else? Talk about the different characters of the buildings we have looked at together."

Next ask the children for their opinions about the building.

> "What do you like and dislike about it? Which of the buildings we have been discussing do you prefer? Can you say why?"

This will will prompt the children to make value judgments about the buildings under discussion. It is interesting to begin talking about the buildings with questions like this and then to repeat them at the end of the discussion. Have any of the children changed their minds? Some of the most exciting discussions are with children who hold opposite points of view and are prepared to argue for them.

All this work on drawing buildings could be adapted as an introduction to the architecture project described in the next chapter.

Materials and Resources:
The actual buildings themselves or photographs

## Designing a building in elevation

The children have experienced or revised some of the foundation exercises on pages 79-81. They may have made an observational drawing of a building or urban landscape. The following sequence of activities should help them design an elevation for an imaginative building of their own.

### ❚❚ A library Search

The library will contain many books that have illustrations or photographs of buildings. Ask the children to search for the best examples. General reference books, books about periods in history and geography books are obvious places to start looking. Story books, illustrated novels and books for younger children can also have excellent illustrations of imaginary buildings. You may want the children to focus on a particular period in history, or perhaps a particular part of the world. Other possibilities include focusing on places of worship, domestic houses and homes or imaginary

buildings. Children might categorise some examples they find under headings that emerge from the discussion about the various purposes or functions of buildings.

Materials and Resources:
The school library
Supplement this project with books from the local library

### ❚❚❚ Collecting examples of window, door and roof shapes

"First of all use your sketchbooks to collect lots of examples of the different window shapes you have found. You may need to draw in some of the smaller shapes that make the inside shapes of the window. Then collect some door and door way shapes and then some roof shapes. Remember that the idea is to collect lots of different kinds of windows, doors and roofs so don't spend too long on any one drawing."

This exercise could be structured so that different groups research a different aspect; one group collects window shapes, another collects door and

A library search

Collecting examples of window, door and roof shapes

## Using the camera to record architectural details from local buildings

The above exercise could be repeated or extended to include examples collected from photographs of windows, doors and roofs taken from buildings local to the school or perhaps from interesting and varied examples of architecture in the town. It is better if the children themselves can be involved in taking the photographs. Further research using books and photographs could involve collecting examples of patterns and other details or features. The children could draw examples in their sketchbooks or even use the photocopier to make individual collections of visual information about buildings.

Materials and Resources:
Camera
Local examples of different buildings and architectural styles
Sketchbooks
Drawing media
Photocopier

doorway shapes and so on. Or perhaps different children within each group could have the responsibility for collecting examples from one or other of the categories. These categories could be extended or reorganised to take into account buildings from different continents or different periods in history.

Materials and Resources:
Sketchbooks and drawing media
Books with photographs and illustrations of buildings

## Talking about different kinds of buildings and their uses

"Why do we need buildings? What are buildings for? What different kinds of buildings are there? What happens inside different buildings? Why are buildings so different one from another? What kinds of

Collecting examples of window, door and roof shapes outside

Research using photographs

buildings are there near the school or near where you live? How could you tell just by looking at a building what it is used for? What kinds of buildings do we live in? What are some of the features that make the school building different from the building you live in? What are some of the differences between a factory and a church? Have you ever been inside any unusual or particularly interesting kinds of buildings?"

It may be useful to make a record of some of the important points that come out of this kind of discussion. A list of all the different categories of buildings will help children make decisions about the type of building they would like to design.

**Materials and Resources:**
Examples of different buildings and architectural styles

## ❚❚ Deciding what kind of building to design

There are some choices to be made. Are the children going to be free to design any kind of building they choose? If the project is closely connected to a theme you may wish to prescribe that the designs are for hospitals, factories, castles, Roman temples, places of worship, domestic houses or maybe for imaginary buildings for characters in a story or novel. What ever the choice, this is a rich opportunity for further discussion and sharing ideas.

## ❚ Looking at an architect's drawing

Most local architects will be only too pleased to lend or give you some copies of their drawings and plans. Ask for a good example of an elevation. You may want to discuss with the children the site plans and maps. There are good links to be made here with map making and scale drawing. It is even better if you have more than one elevation to look at so comparisons can be made. There might also be an opportunity to invite an architect into to the classroom to meet the children or even for a visit to an architect's office. Architects's models might

provide the stimulus for three dimensional work following this design project.

Looking at an architect's drawing might prompt a discussion about different types of drawing and what they are used for. The architect produces drawings for other people to use. Architects also produce drawings that give a client an idea about what the finished building will look like in the context of its site. Artists, on the other hand, might produce very different kinds of drawings of buildings, either real or imaginary.

"What kind of people need to look at an architect's drawing? Let's make a list of the different people who will be involved in building the house to an architect's designs."

Talking about an elevation for a building drawn by a real architect will help the children understand how to work on their own drawing. But it is important that the children have their own ideas and do not simply copy an adult approach.

**Materials and Resources:**
Architects drawings and plans
A visit to an architects office or perhaps an invitation to an architect to visit the school

## ❚❚ Talking about how to get started on the design

"You have lots of information in your sketchbooks, you have the books from the library and the photographs. We have talked a lot about different kinds of buildings. You should have decided what kind of building you are going to design. You only need to think about the front of the building, the elevation, just like the elevations in the architects' drawings we looked at together. You can choose what shapes of windows to use and what shapes of doors or entrances look right for your building. What is the roof going to be like? How many windows will there be? How many doors are sensible? How big is your building? How big are the windows and doors? What other things will you need to include? Think about what the building is used for? How do you think the people who use the building would like it to look?"

You may wish to focus the children on an entirely imaginative idea. For example, after looking at a succession of Italian villas:

"Remember what you said about these buildings. They were magnificent, splendid, huge, amazing, stylish, rich, wonderful, awe inspiring. Now, when you are thinking about the design of your own building, try to make sure that it looks magnificent, grand splendid, huge, amazing, palatial, stylish, rich, wonderful, awe inspiring..."

Example of architectural design, Year 6

Encourage the children to think about any ornamentation that will enhance their building.

**Materials and Resources:**
The sketchbooks
Library books and photographs

## Drawing the design in pencil

At this stage, one approach would be to ask the children to work in rough in their sketchbooks to try out a number of ideas before committing themselves. However, sometimes the class may be so full of ideas that they simply want to get on with their design right away.

The children will be working on large sheets of paper, A2 is ideal. It will be much easier for them if they have drawing boards (see page 123 for more information about drawing boards). Give them HB pencils and tell them they can use any equipment that will help them including rulers, set squares, compasses and even rubbers!

Ask them to work lightly in pencil first because they may need to rub out quite a lot of their drawing before they have a design that they are pleased with.

They should be encouraged to stop from time to time look calmly at their work and discuss it with their colleagues around the table. You might feel it is appropriate to have smaller teams of children,

say three or four per group, working together on a larger design.

It is very important that the children can refer easily to their sketchbooks, the photographs and any other relevant visual information. Remind them about all the possibilities for windows, doors, roofs, patterns and details.

**Materials and Resources:**
Sketchbooks and drawing media
HB pencils
Rulers, compasses, set squares, rubbers
A2 paper
Drawing boards and masking tape or clips

## Finishing the design in ink

"Are you happy with your designs? Have one last look. Is there anything you would like to change? If you have finished you should now draw over your pencil lines in ink. You can use the thin fibre tipped pens. When you have inked up your drawing you can rub out all the pencil marks."

**Materials and Resources:**
Rubbers
Thin fibre tipped pens

## Adding other details

The architect's drawings that the children discussed may have included other details such as trees or drawings of people to give a sense of scale. The children could add these details to their

This architecture project was developed in colour by a group of children using oil pastels, Year 5

designs. Ask them to look carefully at the way the architects drew the extra details and to try to add them into their drawings in the same way. If the building is one for an imaginary character from a story or novel then the extra details could be imaginatively derived from the relevant story.

## ❙Constructing the elevation in card

The children could continue by constructing the elevation in card. Perhaps a whole set of elevations could make a table top town or street. This extension to the project can also be linked to making stage and film sets.

Materials and Resources:
Thin card
Scissors
PVA
Selotape
Drawing and colouring materials

## ❙❙Thinking about colours textures and building materials

This design project does not include work on colour or texture, however the children could go on to consider the appropriate colours and textures for their design which will be linked to the materials from which the building could be made. There is a lot of work that can be done here on building materials and building techniques and a technological focus could become a powerful part of the design project.

## ❙❙Thinking about interiors

Another way to extend the work would be to consider a room or rooms in the building. What kind of fabrics could be used for carpets, curtains and furniture? What would the furniture be like

and how would it be arranged in the room? What would the colour scheme be like? (Ideas for computer aided fabric design are included on pages 36-37. This work on interiors links well to the pattern design project on page 33.)

## ❙Talking about the architecture project and display

Leave the architectural drawings on the drawing boards. Prop them up along a corridor or around the walls of the classroom or hall. Look back to page 85 for ideas about questions that could be asked both about the drawings and the buildings they represent.

"Look carefully at all the drawings. Choose a drawing that you think works well, that looks good. Try to think of a reason for your decision. You might find it difficult to say why you liked the drawing you chose."

Display examples of all the work along side the finished architectural drawings. The photographs, books, photocopied pages from sketchbooks and observational drawings from the previous project will support the child's growing understanding of the design process.

Materials and Resources:
All the children's work from this and other projects related to buildings

Thinking about interiors, Year 4

Ceramic mural, Year 5 and 6

## Starting the mural project

The concept of shape will again provide a foundation for the work. Have the children worked through the sequence of activities that introduce the project on buildings and the built environment? (See pages 79-86.) If they have there will be no need to revise their ideas about shape and they can start by learning or revising how to use clay (see page 73). They can also begin investigating the built environment around the school that will become the subject of a ceramic tile mural.

### ❚ Introducing children to ceramic tiles and murals

The term before this project began, the children in the photographs had visited a local gallery, the Glynn Vivian Art Gallery in Swansea, to see an exhibition of ceramic tiles and tile designs. The visit was organised by the gallery's education officer.

The children made drawings of the tiles in the gallery. This helped them design a motif which they used to decorate a set of four small clay slabs.

Introducing children to ceramic tiles

To save time during the visit the clay slabs had been prepared for them in advance but the class learnt how they could cut shapes out of flat clay, score the underside of the shape and use slip, a mixture of clay and water, to glue the clay shapes on to the small tiles.

To help them understand that a number of tiles could be tessellated to form a much larger design, the same class visited a ceramic tile mural made by other primary school children in the locality.

If it is difficult to find an exhibition or an appropriate example of public art to visit, an alternative would be to phone the visual arts officer for the Regional Arts Association, or Arts Council or try the education officer from a local gallery and ask about ceramic artists in your area who may be able to visit the school.

Materials and Resources:
Sketchbooks and drawing media
Clay pre-rolled into tiles
All the equipment needed for using clay (see page 73)

## Investigating the built environment around the school

Use a camera and sketchbooks to record features of the built environment around the school. Take lots of photographs. These provide a very valuable visual resource for the rest of the project.

> "What do you think are some of the most noticeable features of the neighbourhood? Let's make a list together of what we would see if we walked around the roads and streets."

You could use a map of the local area to help pinpoint remembered landmarks, buildings, factories and so forth.

Investigating the built environment around the school

> "When we go out to draw use your sketchbooks for your research. Make quick, rough drawings of some of the things we discussed, think about shape when you draw. We can often recognise a building or part of a building by its shape."

(For more detailed ideas about drawing buildings, see page 82.)

Materials and Resources:
Sketchbooks and drawing media
Camera
Map of local area

Researching the site of the mural

## Researching the site of the mural

Look closely at the site for the proposed mural. The children can use the sketchbooks to make drawings of the site and they can measure the site. You may wish to go on to make scale drawings. Remind children about ceramic tile murals. Talk about why this site is a good place for a mural.

> "This is where the mural will go when it is finished. What do you think about this site? What is here now? What is it like here? What happens here? What do you think visitors to the school think about this place? Apart from making a mural, what else could we do to improve the site?"

Photograph the site, when the photographs are developed enlarge a print on a photocopier. These photocopies will be helpful in deciding on the size, shape and exact position of the mural.

The children could then be asked to consider the advantages and disadvantages of making a mural from glazed clay tiles. Some examples of tiles are useful to help children answer questions.

"Why are clay tiles good to use for our mural? The mural is going outside. What may happen to the tiles outside? Would paint be better to use for a

Drawings investigating the built environment around the school, Year 5

mural? Let's make a list of the advantages and disadvantages of using ceramic tiles instead of paint. Can you think of any other materials that we might have considered for our mural?".

**Materials and Resources:**

Sketchbooks and drawing media
Camera
Graph paper and equipment for scale drawings

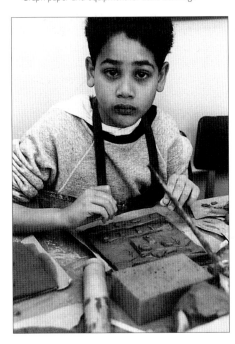

Making
clay tiles

## Making clay tiles and practising making a motif on a single tile

Remind the children both about clay and the equipment they will be using (see pages 73). Lay two wooden slats of even thickness parallel to each other on a wooden board. The distance between the slats will be the width of the tile. In the illustrated project the slats were 6" apart. You may wish to glue or screw the slats in position. The length of the slats should be the same. This helped the children trim the clay so that each tile was 6" square. Cut paper towels to fit between the slats, this prevents the clay sticking to the wood. Use a rolling pin to role out a lump of clay, the rolling pin should be wider than the distance between the slats. The children may need to press more clay into any gaps that appear and re-roll their slab. The smooth, flat slab can now be trimmed.

"Now you can make a clay tile of your own. Every one will need to make two slabs, the first is the tile itself, the base. The second slab will be used to cut shapes out of to decorate the tile. Look at the photos and the sketchbook drawings, use the shapes to help you make a motif on your tile. Don't forget you will need to use the slip to fix each shape on your tile. Remember this is a practice tile."

Individual design for a mural

The children will learn a lot about the problems during this exercise. The emphasis is on practising making the slabs rather than on the quality of the designs. Save some time to talk about the problems the children encountered.

### Materials and Resources:
All the equipment needed for using clay (see page 73)
Wood for boards to help make tiles
Photographs of area and photocopies of sketchbook drawings

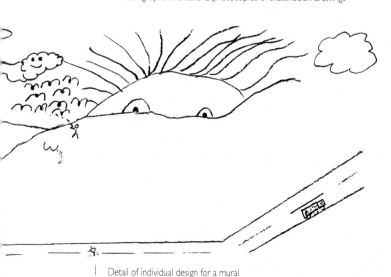

Detail of individual design for a mural

## ◗ Designing the mural

Now that the children understand the some of the problems involved in making relief images on clay tiles they will be better able to think about possible designs.

First of all ask them to think about the size and shape of the mural; use the photocopied photos of the site. You may want the children to make a scale drawing. Ask them to draw a rectangle that represents the shape of the whole mural to scale in their sketchbooks (some children from the class featured in the illustrations chose a circular shape for their mural design). Take the class back to their investigations of the local neighbourhood and ask them to include in their design drawings everything that they think might be important features of the area. The children could do more research by asking adults they know about the characteristics of their neighourhood. The photographs will be very useful reference material.

"Imagine that someone who has never been to this town before is looking at the design. What would you put into your drawing to show what it is like here?"

You may wish to ask other people to help give the children a design brief. Perhaps the parents or governors should have a say about what the designs should show. The headteacher may point out that the money for all the materials is being paid for by the school so he or she should give the children the brief.

Groups of children can discuss their ideas before drawing. If there is time after they have finished their first design, ask them to have another go, making any changes or improvements or perhaps starting on a completely new idea.

The children will be using pencils and rubbers, they may also need to use rulers and compasses.

**Materials and Resources:**
Sketchbooks and drawing media
Maths equipment like rulers and compasses
All the research on the local area

## ❚❚ Voting on the best design

Decide together on the sort of points you might look for when considering whether a design is good or not. Lay out the sketchbooks on the tables and put a letter or number by each book. Ask the children to look carefully and chose their three favourite designs. Ask them to write the letters on a slip of paper, fold the paper and post the voting slip into a ballot box. Count up which three designs have the most votes. Now repeat the process with the three favourites to choose the final winning design.

## ❚ Drawing up a large version of the design

The design will need to be drawn to scale on a large sheet of paper (A1). Square up the small design into the appropriate number of squares, If it is too small, enlarge it on the photocopier. Each square should represent the scale size of one of the clay tiles that will make up the mural. A small group of able children can tackle this, even so they may need some help. It is also possible to

Investigating the built environment around the school

add to or change the winning design at this stage. This West Glamorgan School invited an 'A' level art student from a near-by tertiary college to come in to help the children. This fitted in well with one of the 'A' level design projects at the college and such connections can be very rewarding for all concerned.

**Materials and Resources:**
A1 size paper
A board for support
Drawing media and equipment

## ❚ Making the mural

Making the mural

The mural illustrated in the photos was made in two stages. The final design was squared up into the appropriate number of tiles and photocopied on a large map or plan copier. There were eighty separate tiles in this mural so the school made in advance eighty separate wooden boards with slats. This meant each tile could remain on its own board which helped with the transport and storage of the finished tiles.

The children took over the hall for two days. Builder's polythene covered the floor. The children worked in teams on small sections of the mural. Each team was responsible for rolling out tiles, trimming to shape, and cutting the shaped motifs to add to each tile. The children were asked to think about the best way each team could cooperate. Could different children have different jobs or responsibilities? Was it a good idea to have a team leader to take important decisions or adjudicate if team members disagree?

The most difficult task is to match each tile to its neighbours. Some groups might need a lot of help and you will have to devise a system that allows each group to match the tile they are working on with those that surround it. For the mural illustrated on page 93 children used rulers and dividers to match the width of roads, for example.

The tiles were stored in a cool place to dry very slowly. Each tile shrunk by ten percent as it dried and you may need to allow for this when planning the size of the finished mural.

**Materials and Resources:**
All the equipment for using clay (see page 73)
The final design, copied and squared up

## Firing and glazing the tiles

The school sought professional advice about glazing and firing the tiles. First the children followed the firing of their own practice tiles. After the biscuit firing a simple paint on glaze was used and the tiles were then re-fired. The school asked a professional ceramic sculptor to fix the finished tiles to the outside wall.

A project on this scale would have been impossible without the support of art teachers from the comprehensive and tertiary college, particularly as these institutions provided kiln space and supervised the firing.

## A small scale tiled mural

A small scale ceramic tiled mural could be made for the classroom using the same process outlined above but making fewer tiles. It is possible to leave the tiles unfired. Remind the children how fragile the clay will be when dry and then seal each tile with PVA before painting rather than glazing the tiles. Use a strong glue to fix the tiles to a wooden board for display.

**Materials and Resources:**
All the equipment for using clay (see page 73)
Wooden boards to help make tiles (see page 95)
PVA
Ready mix paint
A wooden board

Example of a tiled mural in school yard, Eastern Primary School, Port Talbot

A gallery workshop, Glynn Vivian Art Gallery, Swansea

## Preparing for the visit

Contact the gallery you wish to visit. Do you need to book your visit? Is there an education officer? Are there any organised projects or activities that you could link with? Are there any special restrictions about the number of children you can take or what activities are allowed when you are there? For example, some galleries will only allow children to work with clipboards or sketchbooks and pencils.

If you are taking the children yourself it is helpful to visit the gallery first to find out about the facilities and what is on show. The gallery visit should be part of a wider project that includes work in the classroom.

### Starting with a look around the exhibition

When the children first see the exhibition they are naturally curious and want to look around. Is it possible to give them a few minutes to look around the exhibition space? Ask them to look out for something particular. For example, ask the children to think about the different people they can see in the paintings. You will need to have an appropriate number of adults to accompany a class. Although supervision in a public space such

as this is an issue, try to give the children a chance to orientate themselves and explore the room they are in before they settle down to more focused work.

### Talking about the gallery

Bring the children together for a discussion. Sit the children on the floor. Ask them to comment on general things first.

> "What are your first impressions of the gallery? What do you think of this exhibition? What have you noticed so far? You were looking out for the different people in the portraits. What have you seen?"

### Talking about a specific painting or series of paintings in the gallery

Discuss with the children the possibilities for more focused work. Can the groups agree which painting or series of paintings they are going to look at more carefully?

### Discussing a particular painting

Children will use ideas from the discussion of a painting to help develop art work back in school. Each group will discuss one painting in the gallery.

Exploring a tactile sculpture, Glynn Vivian Art Gallery, Swansea

Artwork developed after gallery visit and work with 'Ayers Rock'

Artwork developed after gallery visit and work with 'Ayers Rock'

## ❙Making drawings or notes about the painting

The illustrated work was developed after visits to the National Museum of Wales in Cardiff where in the new wing children may only work with sketchbooks and pencils.

The groups were encouraged to collect as much information about the specific painting they had chosen. The children made many written notes as well as small drawings of parts of the painting. They were advised not to try and copy all the painting. It is more worthwhile if they talk to each other about the work and make as many visual or written notes as they can. These can be used to support the children's own art work back in school. (To prompt ideas about how to help the children structure their investigation of the art work look back at pages 57-59.)

**Materials and Resources:**
Sketchbooks or clipboards
Pencils

## ❙Four examples of art made as a response to the gallery visit

Two different school groups chose to discuss 'Ayers Rock' by Michael Andrews. This is a huge representational painting of the famous Australian landmark.

In the first case the children developed work on the rock itself. They developed their own rock

scapes. Teachers used a box of rocks and stones to help stimulate imaginative drawings in pastel. To help them make the drawings they explored the concept of tone (see page 50 for ideas about starting drawing with a focus on tone).

In the second case the children researched Australia in general. They discovered the art work of aboriginal Australians. This became a focus for their own response. The class went on to make a large composite and collaborative fabric design using batik and simple stencilling.

The third example is linked to investigative work on a painting called 'Trees' by Vlaminck. The children went on to develop their own ideas about semi-abstract forests. They made preparatory drawings for a large scale piece called the 'Magic Forest'.

Working from 'Ayers Rock', at the National Museum of Wales

Semi-abstract forest developed after gallery visit and work with trees

The fourth piece was developed after exploring the painting, 'Snowdon from Llanfrothen' by Stanley Spencer. They discussed aspects of the landscape. How had Spencer painted hills, rocks, sky, trees, walls? Back in school the children used oil pastels to make imaginative and individual work prompted by the notes and memories of Spencer's painting. This class were also very taken with 'The Empty Mask' by Magritte. This Surrealist piece is divided into six sections. The children made their own version filling each section with the main features of Spencer's landscape.

Artwork developed after gallery visit in response to Stanley Spencer (see also illustration on page 60)

## An art project away from the classroom

This chapter illustrates how primary school children are able to work on specific art projects organised away from the classroom. In this case the project was called 'An Orchard Environment'. The children visited the Welsh Folk Museum at St. Fagans in Cardiff to work with an artist in the design and construction of an orchard environment. This was part of a special 'Apple Day' celebration.

Other possibilities could include working at the sea shore or working in woodland. Other organisations including the Forestry Commission and National Parks organise projects where children can work in the environment. These can often have an art focus.

### ❚❚ Collecting shapes of trees in sketchbooks

The children used sketchbooks to draw the general shapes of trees in the grounds of the Folk Museum. The discussion focused the children on looking for the particular outline shape of each individual tree. (See page 79 for advice on using the concept of shape to help children draw.) Oak, beech, Scots pine, plane and ash trees were identified for the children. Bark rubbings of each type of tree could be made.

Materials and Resources:
Sketchbooks
Drawing media
Thin paper and wax crayons for rubbings

### ❚❚ Working outside on large drawings of trees

The children worked in an orchard with the artist. The artist helped them to focus on the structure of apple trees. They talked about the scale and texture of the trees.

Large sheets of paper were fixed onto large drawing boards. The children worked with marker pens. They were given the confidence to work on a large scale.

Materials and Resources:
Large drawing supports made from packing case card board
Masking tape
Drawing paper off a roll
Black marker pens

Working outside on large drawings of trees

### ❚❚ Constructing sculptural trees

The children used the large observational drawings as a prompt. They used natural material including witheys, straw, hay, branches, bamboo, string, newspaper and tape to construct sculptural trees.

The artist helped to make the link between the drawn investigations of structure, scale and texture and the same qualities in the sculptural work. The artist also helped the children with different ideas about how to join the natural materials. Often in

Constructing sculptural trees

these situations there is a limited amount of time. The artist and children functioned as collaborators in making sculpture. In some ways the children do not make many creative decisions themselves, they are guided and advised by the artist. However, the experience, as well as the end products, is often very exciting for all concerned. Children gain valuable direct experience of artists and how they make art. This contrasts with the way art is experienced as taught in the classroom.

Materials and Resources:
See text above

## Design an environmental art project

This project is an example of how children can make art work outside linked to the natural environment. Use this as a prompt to design a unit of work that involves investigating and working in the natural environment. Although these children made a visit to take part in this project, there are other ways that you could use work outside to help develop three dimensional making activities back in the classroom.

# Abstraction, construction and relief printing

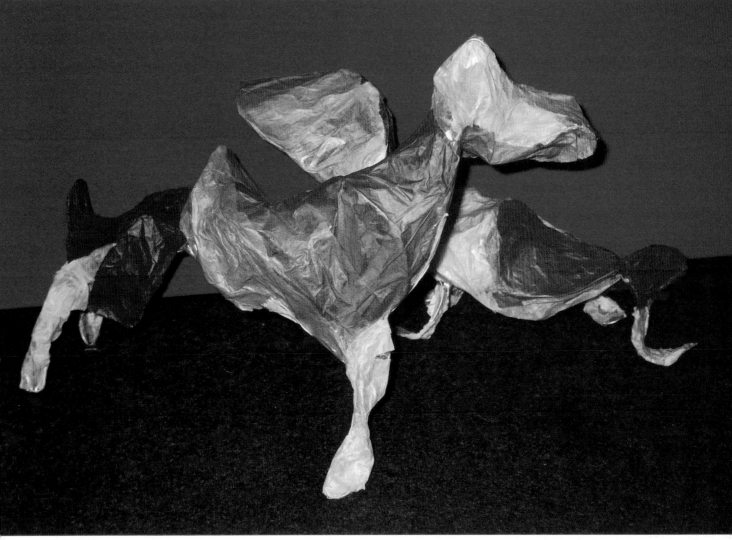

Sculptural dragon, Year 5 (see page 106)

## Lines in wire

The children may have experimented making lines in two dimensions by drawing on paper (see page 51). The start of this unit of work could repeat those exercises. The children will follow this by making lines in three dimensions with wire. This could be called 'drawing in space'.

"Who could make a line with the wire that twists and curls? Can any one show us a way of making a zigzag line with the wire? Who could make a wavy line? Who could make a line that twists and curls? Who has more ideas about other kinds of lines we could make with the wire? Try making the wire turn in a number of different directions. Here is an example, the wire is going away from you, then left, then down, then towards you, then up, then right, then diagonally away from you, then the wire curves around in an arc back towards you again. Try and form the wire in different ways yourselves. Just experiment."

## Exploring how to make shapes with wire

Children could then move on to making shapes with wire. The children will make simple geometric shapes. Ask them to make complicated and unusual shapes. Refer back to shape experiments in the sketchbooks (see page 80).

"I have cut one metre lengths of wire. Experiment to try and find different ways of shaping the wire. Think about how you could make angular or sharp bends. Think about how you could make smooth and curved shapes. Here is some plasticine. You can use this to

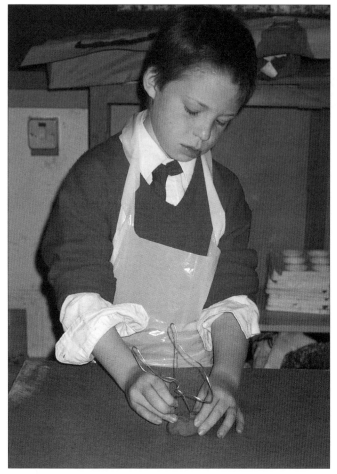

Exploring lines and shapes using wire and plasticine

Ask the children to comment on what they can see. Go on to discuss what the sculpture is made of. Ask the children about the character of the sculpture:

"What does the sculpture remind you of? If the sculpture could come alive how would it behave, what would it do? When you look at the sculpture how does it make you feel? Does the sculpture have a particular character? Think of the words you used to describe your wire experiment. Are any of these appropriate? For example, the sculptures may be sharp, complex, smooth and curved, twisting or angular. The sculpture may look strong or weak, flimsy or delicate. What do you think?"

Ask the children to comment on sculptures they like and dislike. What are the reasons for their comments? This discussion will work the best if children have the opportunity to compare two or more different sculptures.

## ❘Making sculptures

Talk about the problems that they found making the experimental wire shapes. Remember the examples of abstract sculpture. Making abstract sculptures from wire is easier for the children than attempting something that is recognisable. However, if you want the children to work on abstract sculptures you will need to find a specific starting point. The abstract forms could be prompted by starting points that might include experiments with alternative ways of fixing the wire; the concept of balance; exploration of structures or the discussion of abstract twentieth century sculpture. For example, children could attempt their own version of a Calder mobile.

help stand your experiments on the board. As an alternative, after you have bent and shaped the wire, use tape to join the ends together."

The taped wire shapes can be hung as individual sculptures from string in the classroom or combined as part of a collaborative mobile.

Materials and Resources:
Wire that is easy to bend and form cut to 1m lengths
Tape
Plasticine
Boards or cardboard to use as a base or support for the experiments

## ❘Talking about sculpture from the twentieth century

Find illustrations of sculpture from the twentieth century. Much of this work is abstract. For this project abstract or near abstract sculpture is the most appropriate. Many sculptors use wire and metal as well as found objects of all kinds. Artists to look out for include: Picasso, Giacometti, Rodchenko, Moholy-Nagy, Pevsner, Calder, David Smith, Kricke, Caro, Ernst and Philip King.

Better still visit an exhibition of sculpture. An alternative is to seek out examples of contemporary public sculpture in your area.

Exploring lines and shapes using wire

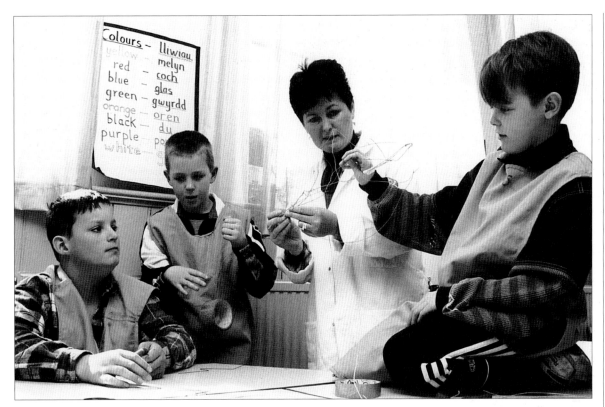

Making the wire structure

Look at the abstract work in two dimensions that grew from discussions about fear (see page 116). The dragon story (see page 23) might provide an excellent starting point for wire sculptures that deliberately attempt to reflect a mood. Of course, if you start with a story about dragons, children will want to go on to make dragons rather than sculptures that convey fierceness. However, the focus on abstract qualities will allow the children scope to try ways of making that are not necessarily hemmed in by a need to produce realistic work.

Manipulating the wire is difficult. The children will work much more easily if they team up as a small group to help each other.

> "You will need to cut different lengths of wire to make your sculpture. Work together. One person can hold the wire whilst another uses wire cutters to cut the length you need. You will also find this soft copper wire useful. Use the thicker wire for the larger outline shapes that make the structure. You could use the copper wire to fill in the more complicated shapes. The copper wire can be twisted and bent more easily. This will help you give the structure three dimensional form. Remember that these are sculptures! Do not just make flat shapes!"

Remind the children about how they can use the tape to join two pieces of wire together. Children will need to be reminded about the need to work carefully and safley with wire (see page 124).

## Making armatures for figures

As an alternative or compliment to abstract work you could show children how to make an armature. Figure work can be linked with figures in clay and figure drawing (see pages 69 and 74).

> "Use one length of wire and bend it in half. Make a twist for the neck as you bend the wire to form a head shape. The two ends become the legs. To make the body put a second twist where the hips would be. You need a second, shorter length of wire for the arms. Twist the arms around the body to join them on at shoulder height."

Materials and Resources:
Wire
Copper wire
Wire cutters
Tape

## Drawing the wire sculptures

Ask the children to make line drawings of their sculptural structures. Use drawing boards, large sheets of paper and drawing media that make strong bold lines.

> "Look around your sculpture. Look at it from different view points. Choose the most interesting angle. Look carefully at the wire lines and shapes."

The children will be committed to drawing the sculptures they have made themselves. Link this

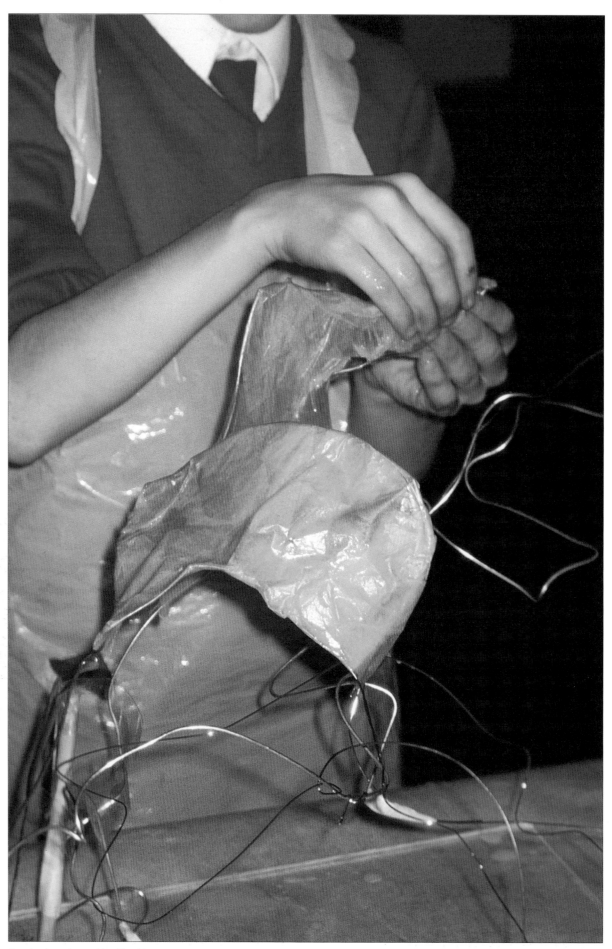

Covering the sculpture with a skin of tissue paper

work to exploration of line (see page 51). Their drawings will look quite abstract. This might be a good time to talk about representational and abstract art.

Materials and Resources:
Drawing boards and masking tape
A2 paper
Black marker pens

## Covering the wire figures

To give form to their figures the children can wrap strips of newspaper around the wire armature. The strips are dipped in a tray of wallpaper or cold water paste. The children should wrap the wet strips around the wire armature, gradually building a solid form.

To speed up the process, children can quickly give the sculptures more bulk by making small parcels of paper. These 'pads' are held in position on the sculpture by wrapping more pasted strips around the figure. It is best to allow several layers to dry overnight before adding further bulk to the sculpture.

Materials and Resources:
The wire armatures
Newspaper
Scissors
Wallpaper or cold water paste

## Covering the abstract sculptures

"First of all use Sellotape to fill in the gaps between the wire lines and shapes that make up your sculpture. It is like adding a skin to an animal. Only do a small section at a time, otherwise the sculpture will get too sticky and cumbersome to work on. Different children in the group can work at different ends of the sculpture.

Cover each area of the taped skin with tissue paper dipped in the wallpaper paste. You can choose the colour of tissue paper for your sculpture. Some of you may want to make multicoloured sculptures."

The children could also use the newspaper technique to give the sculpture a skin. They do not need to use the Sellotape if they choose to work with newspaper strips. They should bind the whole wire skeleton with paper strips dipped in wallpaper paste before adding a skin and building up the bulk as described above. Remind the children to remove excess paste before they add the paper strips to the wire skeleton.

There are many choices and issues at work here. For example, ask the children if they need to cover all the skeleton? Should they leave holes? The sculpture begins to take up volume as the skin is added. Ask the children to discuss how this affects

the look of the sculpture. Does the skin change the character of the object? Children could be given the option of combining their sculptures together. The sculptures will inevitably remind children of animals, creatures and monsters. This can become a topic for discussion and review of the work in progress.

Materials and Resources:
The sculptures
Sellotape
Scissors
Tissue papers in different colours
Wallpaper or cold water paste
Newspaper

Covering the wire with Sellotape

Using plaster bandage to give the sculpture a skin

## Talking about the problems and reviewing the work

Just as with all new techniques the children will soon discover what is easy and what is more difficult to do. Take time to talk over the process with the class. The children soon learn how to improve the way they work.

To start with it is better to plan for small groups to work with adult supervision. As the children become used to the process they will be able to work with increasing independence.

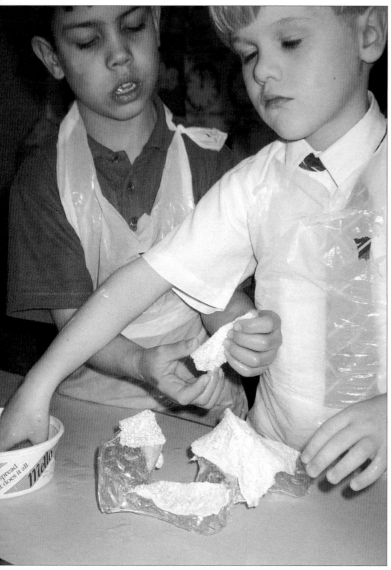

Using plaster bandages

Roc plaster bandage is less messy than either clay or printing in the classroom. Children should work with one length of bandage at a time, soaking each length in a bowl of water for around five seconds. They should let the excess water drip off the plaster bandage before laying it gently over their sculpture. Joins and bumps can be smoothed down with fingers. The plaster soon dries and can be painted.

## Starting points for abstract relief prints

The second approach to abstraction in this chapter focuses upon a technique for making relief prints. Just as with the ideas for sculpture, the prints can be stimulated by experiments with visual elements such as shape, line and pattern (see pages 47-51). Again examples of adult abstract art can also provide an inspiration. For example, artists such as Kandinsky, Klee, Albers, Riley, Rothko, Dubuffet, Pasmore, Nicholson, and Stella use shape in abstract two dimensional work. This is just a representative list, there may well be a young artist local to the school whose abstract painting and drawing might become a focus for the print-making. A great deal of non-representational art from different cultures could also be used as a stimulus for this work.

This printmaking process is a good contrast to the sculptural techniques used in the first part of this chapter. Teachers may want to use such juxtaposition to draw attention to differences between working in two and three dimensions. Planning two related projects in this way will also make it apparent to children just how different are the process used. Each process has its own characteristics, problems, positive and negative points. Children will be understanding how different artists and designers work with a vast range of media and techniques.

Despite the experimental nature of the initial exercises and the unpredictable and abstract look to the end products, children will need good advice and a strong working structure to enable them to take creative decisions about their work. The following sections provide examples of how specific guidance can open up a range of creative options in the work.

Making sculpture in school is space intensive. Where are you going to store the sculptures whilst they are drying? One way is to hang them from string. Perhaps it is worth allocating display space in a public part of the school in advance of the work. The finished sculptures can remain on display for a while. The techniques described here are also suitable for making representational sculptures. Children can use the wire to construct frameworks for sculpture inspired by animals, fish, plants, aliens, machines, monsters and much else.

Use a camera to keep a record the process as well as the finished work.

### Using Mod-Roc to cover the wire sculptures

Use Sellotape to fill gaps between the wire as above. Ask the children to use Mod-Roc as an alternative to tissue paper. Although it is wise to cover tables and floor with polythene, the Mod-

### Working from different sketchbook collections or experiments

Look back to pages 47-51 and search for ideas about making shape, pattern and line experiments and collections. There are a myriad of other

Making relief prints

possible sources for ideas: use the shape examples children collect from the artists they have discovered; natural shapes and patterns discovered in a book on insects; lines developed from sculptural work in wire (look back at page 105).

"Your pattern and shape collections in your sketchbooks included many different kinds of shape. Draw some of the most interesting shapes on to a piece of thin white card or strawboard. Cut the shapes out of the card. Try cutting different kinds of lines out of card. These lines will really be like long thin shapes."

## ◗ Making the relief blocks

"You are going to make a relief print using a thick piece of grey board for the base. You can cut more shapes if needed out of the thinner board.

Use your sketchbooks to plan your abstract design. Think about the work of some of the artists we discussed. Base your design on something you liked. You can look back at the reproductions for ideas. Arrange the shapes and lines you have already cut out on the thick grey board. You can overlap the shapes and lines as much as you like. Until you have made your first print you will not know quite how it will turn out, so feel free to experiment.

When you are happy with the composition you can glue the shapes lines down with PVA.

Use the PVA to coat the relief block, (the grey board

with the shapes glued on). This seals the block you are going to use to make the print. Leave the printing block to dry."

The children can use one cut out shape as a template if they want to repeat the same shape a number of times. You may need to explain what a template is. It is important that the work space is well organised. Look at page 46, where a technique for using glue is described. Adapt this for this printing project.

## ◗ Making the prints

"First of all you will need to choose a colour and then roll out some ink onto this plastic tray. Then roll out the ink onto the block. Cover all one side of the block, that is the raised shapes and the base. Press a piece of paper down over the block to make a print. Use the palm of your hand to press around the edges

Making relief prints

Making relief prints

colour ink on their block and over print the new colour on the paper. They could apply the second colour to selected parts of the block. This will create a contrast between the two colours in the final outcome.

You can make larger class or group prints using this technique. The children can contribute different shapes and ideas to an overall picture or design.

Shapes can be used to create many different designs and pictures. Why not try prints that link to other areas of the curriculum. For example, the prints could have an Aztec theme? Once the children have learnt this technique and discovered some of the possibilities they will be able to make relief prints that have a varied subject matter. How about prints on the theme of fire, air and water? Children will cut out shapes and lines for flames, planes, clouds, waves, boats and much else besides. The arranging of shapes on the block is one way to introduce ideas about composition.

## Talking about and reviewing the finished work

Is there time to talk about the children's work? Storage of finished work is always a problem, especially if work needs time to dry. The children will need somewhere for their prints to dry. The easiest solution is to clear a display board in the classroom. Use drawing pins to pin up each print the children finish. This kind of display is very exciting. Call the board 'work in progress'. The children can see the prints clearly and can easily review what they have done and talk about the problems. The drawing boards may also be useful here. Clip the prints to the boards as the children finish and prop the work up around the walls or along a corridor. This makes an informal exhibition. Again, children can see and discuss their own work and that of other children in the class. Talk about the problems they encountered, ways to improve the processes they used and how the final prints look.

of the raised shapes. Peel the paper off the block and look at your print. You are bound to need some help so team up with a partner so that you can help each other with the prints. Make sure you know where you are going to put the wet print before you start. Try different coloured papers and make a series of prints. Apart from the colour of the paper, is there anything else about the process you could change?"

Ask the children to have a dirty and clean side of their work top. Use fresh sheets of newspaper every time they apply a new coat of ink on the block. Make sure the ink rollers are always returned to the ink trays. The children will find it easier to print in pairs so that they can help each other.

The are many variations to this basic activity. The children could apply ink to all parts of one side of the block, that is to the base as well as to the raised shapes. They could apply ink just to the raised shapes. The children could try making several prints without adding new ink, or they could apply fresh ink each time they make a print. A brush could be used to apply different coloured inks to different raised shapes. When the prints and the blocks are dry, the children can try a new

Materials and Resources:
Sketchbooks
Drawing media
Thin and thick grey board or straw board
Thin white card
Scissors
PVA
Brushes
All the equipment needed for printing:
Water based printing inks
Flat trays for rolling out the ink
Polythene to cover the tables
Damp rags or sponges
Old newspaper
Rollers
A variety of paper to print on

# Sarajevo, war and fear **14**

## A project for older or more advanced children at Key Stage 2

This project is advanced work for Key Stage 2 and may be more appropriate for children in Year 5 and 6. They will need to be confident about their art work. They should be familiar with the visual elements and be used to experimenting and exploring without necessarily always looking for end products.

Here are some pointers as to how advanced the class has become: Are the children using sketchbooks regularly? Are the children drawing with confidence? Are they happy about making 'mistakes', seeing this as just part of how to work at their art? Can you list a number of basic processes such as painting, printing, collage and using clay with which you know the children are confident? Is the class used to talking about art? Are they used to talking about their own art? Are the children fully aware of the visual elements of art, craft and design and are they able to easily refer to them in both their own work an the work of adult artists? Are the children happy to work on a comparatively large scale, say A2 size paper? If there is a positive answer to most of these questions then the class is ready to tackle a project of the following kind.

### ❘ Talking about Sarajevo and the war in Bosnia

Although this project has a Bosnian focus the work could be linked to any town, city, community or people that is suffering in an armed conflict or perhaps from a natural disaster such as earthquake or famine. Another possibility is to link the work to projects about the Second World War. Try starting the work by showing a news clip of a city under attack from snipers. Or perhaps some of the miserable conditions affecting daily life.

"If you lived in Sarajevo or another town in Bosnia what would life be like? What would be happening around you? How would you be feeling? What would you your friends and family be doing? What might have happened to them? How would they be feeling?"

'A man chasing me in my dreams' drawing from Bosnia

Visual notes about
life in Sarajevo

Introduce the concept of civil war. Do the children know of any other civil wars? Do they know where Bosnia is? It might be appropriate to talk about the recent conflict in Northern Ireland and what peace means to the communities there.

Materials and Resources:
A map
News clips, newspaper reports

## Making visual notes about what life is like in Sarajevo.

If you or the children kept a written note of important ideas as they came up during the discussion this could be used to help structure the visual response.

"Now instead of talking about your ideas I am going to ask you to make some drawings that show what you think is going on in Sarajevo, what the people who live there are doing and how they are feeling.

Open your sketchbooks to a double page and cover the pages with lots of small drawings. If you can't draw people very well don't worry too much, you could even use stick men if you wanted! It is the ideas that matter. Some of you may want to write your own notes to go along with your drawings, that's fine too."

You could use large sheets of paper on drawing boards as an alternative to the sketchbooks. Later, the children will enjoy talking about their drawings. This is a good time to emphasise how drawings can be used to record ideas, thoughts and feelings in a rough and immediate way.

Materials and Resources:
Sketchbooks
Drawing media
Drawing boards, masking tape
A2 paper

## Talking about Picasso's painting, 'Guernica'

The painting is widely considered to be a twentieth century masterpiece, showing so clearly the pain, horror and anguish of war. Picasso was responding to the bombing of the town of Guernica in the Spanish civil war. Unusually for paintings, this work is almost monochromatic so a reproduction of it could be photocopied and the children could work from the photocopied reproduction in pairs or small groups. Ask the children to identify what they can see in the painting.

"Now use your sketchbooks to collect some of the shapes that Picasso has used. Remember to include the shapes of some of the things you found when you were talking about what you could see in the painting. Remember not to draw everything in too much detail, it is more important to make a good collection of the different shapes that are shown in the painting."

Now discuss the content of the painting in terms that might include what is happening, what is being felt and what is going to happen next. This is a good opportunity to refer to the initial general discussion about what life might be like in the city. Ask the children for their opinions about 'Guernica'. What do they think about Picasso's style?

"What do you think about this painting? Would you hang it on your wall at home? What do you like and dislike about it? Why do you think Picasso painted it?"

Drawing from Picasso's 'Guernica'

A Year 5 boy commented how much he hated the painting when he first saw it but that now he realised how serious it was and he liked the fact that 'Guernica' really made him think.

Materials and Resources:
Sketchbooks
Drawing media
'Guernica'

## Talking about photographs from newspapers and magazines

Here is an opportunity to introduce children to photo-journalism. Photographs carry powerful messages about war. It is not difficult to resource this from contemporary newspapers and magazines although, obviously, this should be done with some sensitivity. Ask the children to discuss the photographs in the same way that they discussed 'Guernica'. They can go on to compare the painting with the photographs.

"What are the main differences between the painting and the photographs? Which is better, the painting or the photograph? Why?"

Black and white photographs can be used to prompt work on tone. Ask the children to make a version of a part of the photograph using charcoal and chalk or graded drawing pencils. A view finder may be useful. Talk about the effect that either dark or light tones have; perhaps some of the darker photographs look more frightening?

Materials and Resources:
Sketchbooks
Graded drawing pencils
Other drawing media including charcoal and chalk
Off white or buff sugar paper
Hair spray
A collection of black and white newspaper photographs from the war

Talking about photographs from newspapers

## Role play and figure drawing

Ask each group to select one photograph.

"Decide what is happening in the photograph and what the people are feeling or thinking. Work out a very short scene that will show the other groups your interpretation of the photographic image.

Decide what is the most important moment in your scene. Be ready to freeze like statues at that point.

Think carefully about how your bodies are going to show what you are thinking or feeling. What are you going to do with your arms? Are you going to be sitting, standing, lying, kneeling...?"

The children perform and then freeze their role play scene at the most important moment. This is provides a marvellous opportunity for figure

Role play
- praying for the
war to stop

drawing. The rest of the class can use an awareness of shape and tone to draw simple figures posed in expressive and sometimes dramatic ways. The children will have to work fast as the models will soon tire. (A full account of how to help children draw figures is found on page 67-71.)

Materials and Resources:
Look back at the advice about figure drawing (see pages 67-73)

## ❙Discussing fear

It must already be apparent how much of this way of teaching art is married to the English or Welsh language curriculum. Some teachers have commented that working in this way is justifiable entirely in terms of language development and the powerful motivation it provides for children to talk or write about their own feelings.

The project can be developed further by introducing children to adult writing about war. There are many excellent and graphic reports from journalists in Bosnia. There may be an extract from appropriate work of fiction to read at this point.

The focus is now the emotion or feeling of fear. The class can go on to discuss what it is like to feel afraid. Ask the children to talk about their experiences of fear.

> "Have you ever been in frightening situations yourselves? Can you describe what happened? How did you feel? What happens to your body when you are afraid. Is it like being happy and content? What are the main differences?"

It is helpful if children begin to identify words and phrases like: 'shaking', 'goose flesh', 'hair standing up', 'rooted to the spot', 'feeling sick', 'confused', 'empty', 'not knowing what is going to happen next', 'lost' and so forth.

Materials and Resources:
Adult writing about war

## ❙❙Experimenting with colours, shapes, lines and marks to express fear

> "One of you said that when you are afraid you shake with nerves. What kind of mark could you make on the board that looks shaky or nervous? Can anyone else suggest a way of making a mark that could show how they felt when they were afraid?
>
> What colours are usually associated with fear? What colours or combinations of colours go with your sense of fear? Is red the only kind of colour that can show fear?
> Someone else commented that they felt frightened in

claustrophobic - closed in - situations, can anyone think of a way that you could show a feeling of claustrophobia by just using shapes, without drawing a picture? How could you make a shape look nervous? How could you make shapes look confused? I would like you to experiment with different ways of

Collection of the fear experiments displayed in the classroom

showing fear without drawing a picture. You can use shapes, colours, lines and marks and any combination of these. There are different media for you to use, try out different materials for your idea. It is important not to try and draw a picture. First of all experiment with a number of different ideas."

It is better to use large sheets of paper and the drawing boards for this activity. This work is abstract although in a rather literal way. Remind the children about not drawing pictures, encourage them to come up with a range of ideas to start with. Let them use a number of different kinds of drawing media.

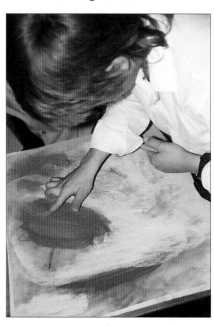

Experimenting with ways of expressing fear

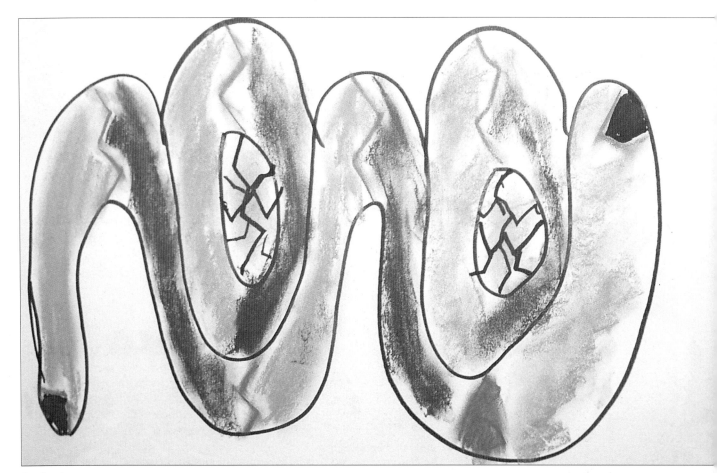

Fear, Year 6

Fear, Year 6

This activity will work well with paint. It is also easily adaptable to a three dimensional exploration using a range of different found materials.

> "Now you have finished the experiments, choose the idea that you think works the best. Use one smaller sheet of paper and draw that idea on its own."

Ask the children to talk about their fear drawings and the thoughts that may lie behind them. Ask the class if they can agree which of the drawings expresses fear in the most powerful way.

Materials and Resources:
Drawing boards, masking tape
A variety of different media

## ❯A final drawing or painting about fear, war or Sarajevo

To recap. If you have followed the structure of the project so far the children will have: talked about the war in Bosnia; made visual notes about what is happening in Sarajevo; discussed Picasso's 'Guernica' and collected shapes from the painting; made tonal copies of black and white photos; talked about journalistic photographs of the war; invented role play scenes; drawn figures from those scenes that express fear; listened to report writing about the war in Bosnia and an extract from an appropriate work of fiction; they have gone on to discuss their own view of fear and experimented with ways of drawing fear using abstract rather than representational motifs. There is much to remember, discuss and look at. The children will have their sketchbooks, 'Guernica', the photographs and drawings. They may well have been involved in creative or factual writing.

> "Think about everything you have done during this project. Look back over all the work. Think up an idea for a drawing or painting that shows something powerful about war in general, life in Bosnia or your own experiences of fear. You can use combine together ideas from any part of the project or just work on making the best of one idea.
>
> You may want to use your sketchbooks to work out what you want to do in rough first."

Some children may produce a powerful visual statement very quickly, others will take hours over their work. It is much the best if you can be flexible about the time individual children use to produce this final piece. Some children may well be motivated enough to work at home.

Materials and Resources:
Sketchbooks
Drawing boards, masking tape
A variety of different media
Visual resources from the project

## A conclusion to the Sarajevo project

This kind of work bridges the gap between Key Stage 2 and Key Stage 3. Art is concerned with expressing ideas and feelings. It is useful in opening channels of communication about deeper thoughts - both for the individual child and the community of the primary class. Important human values can be stressed and through this process children can express opinions about the world as it is presented by the mass media. Projects such as this are founded in issues rather than the more formal strategies for teaching art. It is these formal strategies that form the foundation for many of the projects described in this publication and, in an even more overt way, dominate the activities described in the first book, 'Teaching Art at Key Stage 1'. A fundamental principle behind much of the work described in this publication is that children will have more creative choice and be

The angel of death flying over Sarajevo

'Trapped', Year 6

'My Dearest Home is Burning'

empowered to tackle issues and express more complex ideas and feelings after a formal foundation is in place. When children can work confidently as visual artists they are able to express a great deal through their work. Their confidence can be built through a scheme of work that highlights the visual elements and builds basic knowledge of a simple range skills and processes. Children that have been given a structure that supports visual creativity will be empowered to produce meaningful and expressive art.

## Images from children in Bosnia

The image on this page and the one on page 113 have been made by children who have been brutalised by the actual events of the war in Bosnia. They were made in 1994. The wax pastel drawing, 'My Dearest Home is Burning' is by Mario Zubak, an eleven year old boy from Derventa, Bosnia. Mario is a refugee from the fighting. The drawing is a response to the question, "What do you remember most?". The black and white image, 'A Man Chasing Me in My Dreams' (see page 113), is by Marijana Jurisic´ who was thirteen when she made the drawing. Marijana is from Bushovacha, a small town in central Bosnia. A majority of the school children from the town were refugees. Many had lost their parents, some had witnessed the massacre of their families. The children suffer from nightmares and post-traumatic stress

disorders. Despite the war raging in other parts of Bosnia, the UN protection forces had secured some peace for this town and the elementary school had been kept open throughout the conflict, giving some sense of security to the refugee children. Many of these children find it very difficult to speak about their memories and the fear or horror they experienced. Drawing becomes a powerful and necessary medium of expression. These two images are included as a tribute to all children who have suffered as a result of the conflicts in Bosnia and Croatia.

The images from Bosnia have been reproduced with the permission of Professor Emil-Robert Tanay from the Academy of Fine Arts at the University of Zagreb. Professor Tanay is an art educationalist who has worked a great deal with children who are refugees from the war.

# Conclusion | 15

In the introduction to this book a model was described which interprets the National Curriculum in Art. The National Curriculum is in itself a prescribed model for art education in English and Welsh schools. OFSTED inspectors in England and OHMCI inspectors in Wales will look to see if the school has a policy for teaching art and how that policy is implemented in the classroom through a planned scheme of work. There is enormous pressure to plan for art. Structures and models that make that planning easier and time efficient are useful tools for the class teacher who may very well not be a specialist in the subject.

The introduction also advocated the importance of paying attention to the particular nature of each art activity. By doing this it is possible to describe how art works in a way that makes it accessible to all teachers and children. Art and design is not a special, mysterious subject but something that effects our lives in a down to earth, day to day kind of way. Paying attention to the detail of how art works in each case is paying attention to the richness of a subject that reflects the richness of being alive.

There is an apparent contradiction between the need to use models and systems that generalise art activity and the nature of that activity, which seems to be so particular that the only sensible way to make it clear is to describe how each potential activity works in detail.

There are dangers. The first is to assume that any model or system is the only model or system that can be applied. The National Curriculum in Art is a document from a specific period of our history. It reflects the political and cultural conditions of our time. Art educationalists (or civil servants) would have written a different document fifteen years before and will write a different one fifteen years into the future. Models and systems are not writ in stone but tools, very useful tools, to help plan the teaching of a subject that is confusing in its diversity and breadth. However, while the model or system is a tool for planning, it does not in itself guarantee the quality of the art activity from either the teacher's or the child's point of view.

Another danger is to blindly use specific descriptions of successful art activities as a recipe that can be repeated again and again. The nature of art means that the results of an activity, indeed the activity itself, is different in each case. The projects described in this book worked; they have all be 'tested' in the classroom. Teachers will find much that can be incorporated and adapted for their own art projects, in their own classrooms. The specific details of what may be said to children will prompt teachers to make similar points to their own class. However, each time a teacher sets out to help a group of children different words will be used. Each child, in every single case, will make a response that is unique. So the National Curriculum in Art is a curriculum model limited by cultural and political conditions and the document remains lifeless, some would say useless, without detailed examples of how art works in the classroom. In contrast 'how to do it' activity books (recipes that guarantee an end product for the walls) miss the point about how art works and deny each child's right to work through art to explore and express their own individual sense of their world.

This book places before teachers a set of examples that describe how art can work in the primary classroom. These show the value of allowing each child to explore and experiment; the need to build a foundation of basic skills; the vital role that the visual elements of art have in helping children to understand how art works; and the importance of investigating the context for the activity by examining the subject or theme that prompted the work. Talking with children about art and about making art, talking with children about the context that gives meaning to their art is vital to this model. The chapters in this book describe an application of these ideas in the classroom. The projects are intended as examples that contribute towards an art eduction in primary schools that produces confident and creative children who have the means to express their ideas and feelings about the world. Art education can only succeed if there is symbiotic relationship between theory and practice.

'Trapped by Fear', Year 6 (see page 118)

# Equipment and materials check list

This is a list of the equipment and materials you will need to complete all the projects in this book. This list could be used as the basis of a checklist to ensure that a foundation for art, craft and design is resourced in the school. This cannot claim to be a comprehensive list. There are numerous other possible projects and processes.

## Equipment

Drawing boards
   (these are essential - make out of thin plywood large enough to hold an A2 sheet of paper. The drawing boards illustrated in the text were made from sheets of 8'x4' 1/8th" ply cut to 10 pieces of 19" x 24". The edges should be sanded or taped. Ideally corners should be rounded and the boards varnished.)

Bulldog clips
Drawing pins
A staple gun
View finders
   (Small sheets of card with various sizes of rectangle cut out of the centre)
A camera
Magnifying glass
Computer draw and paint software
Easels
Scissors
Glue containers
Glue spreaders
Rollers
Hole punch
Wire cutters
Folders or portfolios for children's work
Rulers
Set squares
Compasses
Rubbers
Clay tools and lollipop pop sticks
Clay boards
Containers for slip
Wooden boards to help form clay tiles
Rolling pins
Sponges
Rags
Mixing palettes (flat)
Paint palettes
Containers for water
A selection of brushes
   (thick and thin, try: round head size 4 and 10; flat head size 6 and 12; a fine tipped soft brush size 4; household 1/2" brushes)
A paper cutter

Cutting knife
Old shirts or aprons
A collection of natural and made materials
   (e.g. collect objects with interesting textures)

## Consumable Materials

Roll of thin builders polythene
Masking tape
Sketchbooks
4B pencils
HB pencils
H pencils
Charcoal
Chalk
Soft pastels
Oil pastels
Fibre tipped pens
Coloured marker pens
Coloured pencils
Coloured felt pens
Black wax crayons
Coloured wax crayons
Fixative (use cheap firm hold hair spray)
A1, A2, A3, A4, A5, A6 cartridge paper
A1, A2, A3, A4, A5, A6 cheaper drawing paper
   (e.g. newsprint)
Grey and off white sugar papers
Coloured sugar papers
Tissue paper
Tracing paper
Roll of cheap paper
Cardboard
Raffia and string
Sellotape
Wire
Copper wire
Thick and thin grey board or straw board
   (use to make relief prints)
Art straws
Polystyrene tiles
   (e.g. Pressprint from Berol)
Old newspapers
Old colour magazines
Junk cardboard
Wallpaper paste
PVA glue (Marvin Medium)
Water based printing inks in different colours
Water based school paint
   (it is useful to have both powder and ready-mix paint in stock - you will need a collection of colours that allows children to fully explore the possibilities of colour mixing, try: bright blue, turquoise, crimson, bright red, yellow ochre, bright yellow, white and black)

Other paint
  (e.g. water colours, acrylics, oil paint - these can
  be expensive so must be optional)
Special printer cartridges or paper
  (that allow children to transfer designs from the
  computer onto fabric)
Washing up liquid
White spirit
  (not for the children to use)
Plasticene
Clay
  (use school grey clay or red earthenware, use
  the grey clay if you are going to glaze or paint
  the ceramic objects in bright colours. Use
  grogged clay if you are making ceramic tiles for
  outside)
Paper bags
Plaster bandage
Natural materials for making sculpture or weavings
  (Reeds, straw, twigs and branches etc.)
Cheap white fabric
Coloured fabric off cuts
Fabric crayons, paints and pens

## Examples of art, craft and design

Schools will also need a collection of images of
adult, art, craft and design that includes historical
and contemporary examples and examples from
many different cultures. It is often forgotten that
there is a wealth of design around us all the time.
If appropriate, use examples of fashion, fabrics,
interior decoration, cars, gardens, architecture,
book illustrations, ceramic items, kitchen utensils,
light fittings, jewellery, household appliances,
motorway bridges, door furniture, chairs and so on.

There are many commercial postcard and poster
packs on the market that will provide a cross
section of fine art images - the emphasis is firmly
on historical examples of Western European art.
Discount book shops often have very inexpensive
art books and posters.

There are a number of ways of collecting images
for free. Collaborate with your colleagues to
collect old postcards, calenders, photos from
magazines, birthday cards and so on (don't forget
to include images of design and art from different
cultures). Make sure the school is on the mailing
list of a number of art galleries - you may receive
invitation cards that have images and even posters.
Three dimensional art is often difficult to introduce
using reproductions. Use the examples of public
art in your area. Churches and other places of
worship often contain beautiful art objects. Some
schools build a commitment to visit art galleries
into their art policy; a local art gallery may have an
education officer who will offer advice. It may be
possible to visit an artist's studio or workshop.

There has been a rapid growth in the number of
artist in school projects over recent years. These
are organised by outside agencies or by the school
themselves. Is there a parent who is an artist,
craftsworker or designer perhaps they could be
invited to visit the school?

There will be an increasing number of commercially
available CD ROM collections. As schools become
connected to the Internet they will be able to
access huge numbers of relevant images..

Look out for examples of contemporary art. Be
open minded - it is not necessarily the most
popular examples of art (Van Gogh, Monet etc.)
that provide the most exciting stimulus for children.

## Health and safety

All the projects included in 'Teaching Art at Key
Stage 2' have been tested in the classroom and to
the best of our knowledge are appropriate in the
primary school. However, as with all practical
activities care should be taken with the use of all
materials and equipment. For example, using wire
(see page 107) could be dangerous if children are
not warned about potential problems and taught
to act sensibly and safely in the classroom. It is the
teachers responsibility to ensure this. A book. 'A
Guide to Safe Practice in Art and Design',
produced by the Department of Education and
published by HMSO is available from the NSEAD
(01249) 714825 at £6 including postage and packing.

## The National Society for Education in Art and Design

The **National Society for Education in Art and Design** is the leading national authority in the United Kingdom, combining professional association and trade union functions, which represents every facet of art, craft and design in education. Its authority is partly based upon a century-long concern for the subject, established contacts within government and local authority departments, and a breadth of membership drawn from every sector of education from the primary school to universities. The unique membership position of the Society makes it the only educational organisation which is able to draw on opinions of practising experts and to promote policies for, and on behalf of, all sectors of education in one specific subject area. The Society is an independent trade union within the meaning of section 30 of the Trades Union and Labour Relations Act 1974.

The NSEAD's roots can be traced to 1888, when a group of art school principals, who felt the need to raise the standard of art teaching and improve the status of art teachers, founded the **Society of Art Masters.** With the development of art and crafts as part of general education, and the appointment of men and women as full-time specialist art teachers in schools, the membership was extended and, in 1944, the Society adopted the title **National Society for Art Education.**

Another strand of the Society's history concerns the **Society for Education through Art** which grew out of a framework of an institute for exploring new ideas in art and education, proposed by Henry Moore, Eric Gill, Herbert Read and Alexander Barclay Russell. The **SEA** itself was formed in 1940 by the amalagamation of the **Art Teachers Guild** and the **New Society of Art Teachers.** After two years of negotiations the **SEA** and the **NSEAD** merged their interests to become the **National Society for Education in Art and Design** in 1984.

## Primary sector corporate members

Although primary school teachers are eligible for individual full membership of the Society, recently a new membership category has been introduced whereby primary schools may become corporate members of the NSEAD on payment of much reduced subscription (33%). This category of membership is available to schools which cater in part or whole for children between the ages of 3 and 11 years and those from which children have left before their fourteenth birthday. Membership will be vested in a school representative - usually the headteacher or the art coordinator. The benefits include regular mailings of NSEAD periodicals with up-to-date information on developments in the field, information on the Society's expanding InSET programme (much of which is aimed at the primary sector), and reduced registration fees for NSEAD conferences.

Further information and application forms are available from:
NSEAD, The Gate House, Corsham Court, Corsham, Wiltshire, SN13 0BZ
Tel: 01249 714825   Fax: 01249 716138

| TITLE | PRICE |
|---|---|
| **NSEAD PUBLICATIONS**<br>**TEACHING YOUR CHILDREN ART**<br>A Handbook for Teachers and Parents. Colour, Texture, Painting<br>Nigel Meager | **£4.50** |
| **TEACHING ART AT KEY STAGE 1**<br>Nigel Meager | **£11.95** |
| **A YEAR IN THE ART OF A PRIMARY SCHOOL**<br>Robert Clement & Liz Tarr | **£16.30** |
| **ART MACHINE**<br>Edited by Arthur Hughes, Nick Stanley and John Swift | **£5.20** |
| **DEPICTIONS OF AN ODYSSEY**<br>Peter MacKarrell, edited by Sheila Paine | **£11.80** |
| **A GUIDE TO COURSES & CAREERS IN ART, CRAFT AND DESIGN:**<br>Creative Futures | **£15.00** |
| **ART EDUCATION AND MULTICULTURALISM**<br>Rachel Mason | **£14.50** |
| **IMPROVING YOUR SCHOOL ENVIRONMENT - PIONEERS**<br>Nick Clements and Sarah Osborne | **£12.00** |
| **DESIGNS WE LIVE BY**<br>Helga Loeb, Phil Slight and Nick Stanley | **£12.00** |
| **TEACHING YOUR CHILDREN ART**<br>A Handbook for Teachers and Parents. line, Shape and Drawing<br>Nigel Meager | **£4.50** |

*For a full list of publications available and current prices –*
*check our wesite at www.nsead.org*

## ALL PRICES INCLUDE POSTAGE & PACKING

**NSEAD, The Gatehouse, Corsham Court, Corsham, Wiltshire SN13 0BZ**
**Tel: 01249 714825  Fax: 01249 716138**

Printed by Pensord Press Ltd., Tram Road, Pontllanfraith, Blackwood, Gwent NP2 2YA

# Notes

## Acknowledgments

The following is a list of schools who have in one way or another worked with the authors and in doing so made contributions to the development of the ideas that form the content of this book. We would particularly like to acknowledge the support of South Glamorgan's Local Education Authority. Nearly all these schools are from Wales, notably from South Glamorgan, West Glamorgan and Gwynedd.

Adamsdown Primary, Albany Primary, Ammanford Juniors, Ardudwy Cluster, Arfryn Primary, Blaen Baglan Primar, Blaenymaes Primary, Bryn Deri Primary, Cadoxton Juniors, Cadle Primary, Catwg Primary, Cefn Onn Primary, Clase Junior, Classyc's Consortium, Clwyd Primary, Cogan Primary, Craigcefnparc Primary, Craigfelin Primary, Eastern Primary, Fairwater Primary, Felindre Primary, Ffaldau Primary, Gladstone Infants, Gladstone Primary, Glan-yr-Afon Infants, Glan-yr-Afon Juniors, Grange Primary, Gwyrosydd Infants, Haresfield Primary, Holton Junior, Jenner Park Primary, Llandough Primary, Llanedeyrn Primary, Malborough Infants, Marlborough Juniors, Millbank Primary, Palmerston Primary, Pentrepoeth Juniors, Portmead Primary, Radnor Primary, Rhiwbeina Juniors, Rhydypenau Primary, St Bernadette's R.C. Primary, St

Cadoc's R.C., St John Lloyd R.C. Primary, St Mary's R.C. Primary, St Philip Evans R.C. Primary, St Thomas Primary, Stacey Primary, Sully Primary, Ysgol Treganna, Ysgol Cefn Coch, Ysgol Coed y Gof, Ysgol Croesr, Ysgol Dyffryn Ardudwy, Ysgol Llanbedr, Ysgol Penrhyndeudraeth, Ysgol Tan y Castell, Ysgol Talsarnau, Ysgol Traeth - Abermaw, YsgolY Garreg - Llanfrothen, Ysgol Y Wern.

The following schools were also involved at the St Fagan's Welsh Folk Museum Activities Week (see Chapter 12): Bishop Childs C.W. Primary, Cefn Wood Primary, Gelli Primary, Pant Ysgallog Primary, Pontllanfraith Junior, Radnor Primary, St Francis R.C. Junior, St John Lloyd R.C. Primary, St Philip Evans R.C. Primary, Tongwynlais Primary, Y Bontfaen Primary.

We would also like to thank:
Pat Arlott, Ceri Barclay, Mike and Barbara Collier, Andy Dark, Julian Davies, Liz Davies, Helen Evans, Gillian Figg, Selwyn Gale, Anne Ingall, Tony Lloyd, Roger Meager, Julien Morton, David Petts, John Rowlands, Sue Snell, Dr Derek Stears, Dr John Steers, Professor Tanay, Stephen Verbeeck, Tina Watkins, Welsh Folk Museum, Mike Yeomans.